The Way It Was!

The Way It Was!

Walter H. Adams, Sr.

VANTAGE PRESS
New York

Published by Vantage Press, Inc.
419 Park Ave. South, New York, NY 10016

Manufactured in the United States of America
ISBN: 0-533-15366-2

Library of Congress Catalog Card No.: 2005908778

0 9 8 7 6 5 4 3 2 1

To all of my children and grandchildren.
I hope that throughout their lifetimes they will never ever
have to question things that I have done in my lifetime.
I know that the truth hurts, but I also know that it has set me
free.
Last, but not least, I want to thank all my friends for really
believing in me and never giving up hope that I would truly finish
this.

Contents

The Theme or Premise

I believe every family that grew up in a village setting, living off the land, can relate to this.

Those Trying Times

Out of work with no money coming in
Not a penny to my name
With a wife and children to feed
We were happy, just the same
Money was the least of our worries
At least it was in my day and time
Times were tough all over, so there's
Really no one to blame
We were blessed beyond our wildest dreams
With moose and deer and salmon in the streams
Because jobs were scarce and hard to get
It seems we were always in great debt
To the local store for giving us all credit.
I loved and cherished the simple lifestyle
We can now look back at those "good old days"
As a test of faith which seems to say
We have weathered the storm, and beat the odds
When the odds were not in our favor
Oh, but the memories of those trying times
We will always and forever savor
Life is just one big struggle after another
We're just trying our best to survive
In a world where survival of the fittest
Is the name of life's game.

Preface

If anyone asked me a few years ago if I planned to write my life's story, I would have laughed in their face. But when I reflected back on my life, I always had this desire to tell stories about incidents and episodes that happened in my childhood; so I figured why not put it on paper and see what happens.

I found out soon enough that there was a difference between telling a story, and writing it in some meaningful format. However, as I continued to struggle with my expressions, I began to have doubts about whether I should continue.

One day I read an article in the *Reader's Digest* by best-selling author Tom Clancy. What he had to say about writing really inspired me to continue. He said, "Writing is like golf or skeet shooting and any other human endeavor; the only way to do it is to do it!" He continues, "What success really means is looking failure in the face and tossing the dice away. You may be the only person who ever knows how the dice came up, but in that knowledge you have something that millions of people will never have—because they were afraid to try!" I told myself I was going to continue to try!

When I tell someone that I am writing my story, I'm often asked "Why are you writing a story about your life?" My reply has been, "Why not?"

You know, there is a saying about laughter being the best medicine for whatever ails you. I believe this very strongly. However, I'd like to add that a person has to be happy and content from the heart with him or herself before one can really laugh at themselves. I have always lived by the saying, "If you can't laugh at yourself, who can you laugh at?" There are far too many people who are laughing on the outside, but crying for attention on the inside. It is these people I hope to reach and touch. If I can inspire a reader to laugh at themselves, no matter how many obstacles one might have to overcome with life's struggles, then I have accomplished my task, and that's all I can ask.

Growing up in a small fishing village in northern Southeast Alaska during the 1940s and 50s in an area I like to refer to as "God's Country" has instilled in me a true love of nature, the animals, and of all mankind, as we struggle for survival to live as one with nature in all its unique and mysterious ways.

Throughout my childhood I grew up living a "subsistence" lifestyle—living off the traditional Native foods like clams, cockles, seaweed, seal meat, herring eggs, deer, moose, ducks, geese, and all the different varieties of fish you can imagine. I never realized how important this lifestyle was until I started to raise a family of my own. It suddenly became apparent to me that times and laws were changing! In order to gather our Native foods we now have to have a license, or obtain a permit; there are also limits as to how much and when you can gather certain foods. I have always felt unique and special, as I would relate a story to my children about how I used to love to drink seal oil, or eat sea urchin eggs, as we picked them out of the shallows, or opened a cockle to eat raw. I could go on and on, but times have changed and it's a great shame.

I have returned to my hometown of Yakutat only once since leaving in 1965. In 1971 I flew to Yakutat to hunt moose, but the weather was terrible so I left after only three days.

I would like to go to Dry Bay and Akwe someday, just to see if there are any of our cabins in the area.

Memories are all I have left.

The Way It Was!

I believe my first real memory of any importance as a child was when the war ended in 1945.

I Remember It Well

I was only 4 1/2 years old at the time, but I remember it well.
Sirens were blaring and people were dancing in the street.
The war was finally over, or at least this one was,
for a short spell.
No more lights out at eight, or curfew, or sirens to hear
And the town generator would stay on 'til midnight or so.
We never had it so good since I don't know when.
There was a dance on the dock that lasted all night, I know.
To me it was like New Year's and the 4th of July, all combined.
For days afterwards, there was pastry and candy
and pop, free for the taking.
'Cause it took the whole town a couple of days to unwind.
This is how I remember the day the war ended.
In 1945, in Yakutat, Alaska, where I was raised.
Though I was only 4 1/2 at the time, I remember it well.

1

The Growing Years

"The war is over! The war is over!" We heard the words blend with the wail of the village air-raid siren. Mom was pouring hot water from a kettle into a basin in the sink over dirty dishes. "Fire!" she said. I got up from the floor where I was playing marbles and looked out the window. I looked down on the dock where I had seen some older men visiting and throwing a line over the dock, fishing for halibut.

At the same time we heard Bert shout from upstairs, "What's that?" Earlier, he and I were both upstairs—he was working on a model airplane and I was pestering him to let me help him. Mom had called me downstairs when she heard us quarreling and starting to fight. "What's going on, Mom?" Bert asked.

"Don't know," Mom said as she replaced the kettle back on the stove. Steam came from the sink and fogged the mirror hanging above it. "Maybe it's an air raid," she said, walking over to the window and looking down at the dock. People were looking around as if they were wondering what was happening.

"The war is over!" We heard the words repeated. When the siren ebbed, the airport siren, located five miles away, began the process all over again.

"The war is over!" she said. Soon both sirens wailed simultaneously, drowning the shouts of the townsfolk as they came out of their homes amidst the festive atmosphere. It was like the Fourth of July and New Year's celebration all at the same time.

We heard what sounded like rifle shots coming from the trail atop the hill above our house.

People on the dock began to shout, "Yippee! Hooray!"

Another person hollered, "God Bless America!"

It seemed like an eternity, but when both sirens finally faded, then stopped, people continued to celebrate while they headed for the dock, which was the customary gathering place whenever anything eventful happened.

"Knock knock!" It was my friend, Joe Nelson. "The whole town's going to the dock to see what's happening." Joe had a slight lisp when he talked; his cap lay crookedly on his head so the brim covered his right ear. Hanging around his neck was his trusty slingshot. He had been on his way over to see if I could play outside, but had gotten caught up in the excitement about the war being over. Joe was a year older than I.

My brother, Bert, came running down the stairs from the second story of our house, which was located right in the middle of town overlooking Monti Bay. "Did we win?" he asked Mom. "Did we win the war, Mom?" His eyes were as round as an owl and shining with enthusiasm.

"Yes," Mom answered, taking out a pie from the oven of the oil stove. "I think we won. Pops, let Joe inside," my mother said. She had been busy all morning making bread and apple pies.

Joe came in, his ankle-length boots flopping on the floor. "Wanna come?" he asked. I couldn't help but notice that he carried all the accouterments of a real friend. Looped around his belt was a bag full of marbles. I looked at Mom with my quizzical look and before I even asked, she said, "Let's all go down. Just give me a minute while I take the bread out of the oven."

Soon Mom, my brother, Bert, Joe and I were in the crowd walking to the dock. The wail of the sirens gave way to the noise of the military trucks arriving from the airport. There were about 10,000 military personnel stationed in Yakutat compared to the town's population of about 300, so we knew the dock area would be crowded soon.

As we neared the dock Mom told us to wait for her while she ran into the store where the only telephone in town was, to call the army base and see if Dad was going to be let off work. She returned a short time later.

"Dad should be coming in on the bus anytime now," she said.

We waited by the end of the warehouse on the dock for him. Someone was talking through a megaphone at the entrance of the dock where the majority of the people had gathered.

Joe found his parents and was soon lost in the swelling crowd, which by this time was chaotic.

"The war is over! The war is over!" We heard the announcement over the megaphone. "Beginning immediately, there will be no more curfews and the town power plant will stay on all night every night." This meant that there would be an end to the blackouts and false air raids.

Dad eventually found us and he hoisted me to his shoulders. Mom took Bert's hand so we wouldn't separate and get lost in the crowd. A soldier was handing out beer to the adults and soda pop to the kids. We made our way to the end of the dock where local musicians were setting up for a dance.

"Maybe we'd better get back home soon," Bert said. "Mom and Dad are starting to drink." The dance on the dock was getting underway. A concession area was established alongside the warehouse on the dock where food, soda pop, and beer were managed. Bert and I each had two bottles of Coca Cola and we found a paper bag to fill with pastries and canned rations the military had set out in the concession area. By the time Bert and I headed home, we each had a bag full of goodies. The dance lasted all night long and the noise of the partying was so loud that my brother and I didn't get much sleep at all.

Bert was three years older than L but whenever our mom and dad started drinking he always seemed to grow up. He took care of me, and I looked up to him in times of crisis because I knew he would do a good job of it. Except for this one time—an episode that had scared him and Mom and Dad and the whole community.

At the bottom of the stairs on the end of the cannery store there was a large dog house. The previous summer I had been playing hide and seek with about eight friends, when I kicked the dog out of his house and crawled into it to hide. When the other kids couldn't find me they just took it for granted that I had gone home. Bert had been home working on a model airplane all afternoon, so when my friends headed home after the game, they stopped by my house to ask why I had gone home. Mom heard them asking about me and told them that I hadn't come home. She had assumed I was still out playing with them. Mom became frantic, thinking that I had either fallen off the dock or had been hurt and was unable to come home. She scolded Bert for not being with me to take care of me then sent him out to look for me. When Bert came back in a half hour or so without me, she sent him back out to organize a search party of his friends to continue the search.

Meanwhile, Mom went to use the town's only telephone at the cannery store to call Dad. Dad worked for the Army at the base five miles from town. It was about three o'clock in the afternoon and no one had seen me since about one o'clock. Dad rushed home from work and immediately organized a group of his army friends and people from town with skiffs to drag the shoreline and comb the beaches for me. My friends were searching the beach under the cannery, calling, "Popeye, where are you? Popeye can you hear me?"

All this time everyone ignored the store manager's wiener dog barking furiously outside the dog house.

The search continued for about three and a half hours until the cannery mechanic shouted, "Here he is! He's sound asleep in the dog house!"

I could just picture myself sitting in that dog house rubbing sleep from my eyes, completely unaware that my parents had practically the whole town and army base looking for me. When my dad got to me, he lifted me and slid me on his shoulders and took me home. To this day I remember the concerned look on my mother's face, but the one that got me was the fear in my brother's. I was still on my dad's shoulders when we entered our house. Bert ran to us and hugged Dad and said, "You found him like you said you would and he's alive."

I was constantly teased by my friends and relatives about that incident for months afterwards, but I could tell that Bert didn't appreciate that much. I guess it was because he always felt responsible for me and this was the first time in his eight-year-old life that he had lost control of that responsibility.

To remember the past, as if it were yesterday, is a true sign that it must have been wonderful.

Memories

My heart yearns to go back home just one more time
To see the beautiful land where I was raised
Nestled between two giant mountains of great notoriety
The beautiful Mt. St. Elias and Mt. Fairweather
The wide-open spaces in between what I call God's country
In the heartland of northern Southeast Alaska.
It boasts over 100 miles of sandy beach along its coastline
With the pounding waves of the Pacific Ocean ever present.
It is not the town of Yakutat itself I wish to see
But the rivers and streams in the outlying area for me
Hold so many memories of days gone by so dear to my heart
A cabin in the Alsek River where we wintered in '47
And a log cabin we built on the banks of the Akwe in '58
Where we fished and hunted every summer for ten whole years
Sometimes the memories seem like it was just yesterday
But it's been closer to fifty years ago already
When the way it was is now the way it used to be
When we lived off the land in God's country.

2

Mother's Family Tree

Far into the interior of Canada is the Tatshenshine River system. The Alsek River breaks off from this system and passes over the border into Alaska and widens out as it drains into Dry Bay. Dry Bay, in turn, drains into the Gulf of Alaska about sixty-five miles from Yakutat, along the coastline.

On the Akwe River, about twelve miles toward Yakutat, is where my mother's family came from. I'm told my mother's family used to trade with the different tribes from the interior Port of Alaska by means of the Alsek River. It was through this trade route that my mother's family settled in the Dry Bay area in the mid-1800s.

My grandmother's name was Esther Johnson, a full-blooded Tlingit who was born in Yakutat, Alaska, probably around 1900 or so.

My grandfather's name was Charlie Johnson. He came from Karlscrona, Sweden. He was full-blooded Swede.

He was in the Royal Swedish Navy, and on the day his enlistment was up his ship was tied up at the dock in Yakutat, Alaska. He got off ship and made Alaska his home from that very day. He soon met my grandmother and fell in love.

Charlie and my grandmother had two children together before they were married. Lorraine was born on November 24, 1915, and my mother, Stella, was born on July 8, 1917. In 1918, Charlie and Esther finally married. He moved his family to Dry

Bay where he ran a store from a scow, and smoked and salted king salmon. On September 23, 1919, Daisy was born.

Charlie eventually moved to Hoonah where he started a shipyard with a friend. During the spring, he would tow his scow with his trolling boat, the fishing vessel *Verdi*, to Dry Bay and spend the summers salting king salmon and commercial fish for sockeye and silver salmon. He would not return home until the season was over in October. While gone one summer, a youngest daughter, Agnes, was born, but she contracted the flu and died when she was just a few weeks old. Not too long afterward Esther, too, died from the same disease. Because there were no telephones or other sources of communication, when Charlie returned home after fishing, he found all his children living with friends.

He found out soon enough that he not only lost his wife, but also a daughter he never even saw. He was so distraught, and had no recourse but to send all his children to attend school at Sheldon Jackson in Sitka, Alaska.

Mother was of small stature, about five foot two inches tall, with light brown hair always curled up on the back and sides. She had brown eyes, with a prominent nose, and was fair skinned. She used to tan easily in the sun, and even her hair used to have a reddish tinge to it in the summer time. As a young girl she always called Yakutat her home even though she lived in Hoonah for a time, and at Bethel Beach Home in Juneau, Alaska.

During the winter months, Mom and her sisters attended school at Sheldon Jackson. Mom graduated in 1936, and eloped on the day of her graduation with my brother's dad, John J. James, of Sitka, Alaska. They made their home in Sitka, and just three months before Bert was born. His dad and a brother, as well as two other family members, all drowned while on a hunting trip near Sitka, Alaska. Bert was born on February 4, 1937.

My mother remarried about a year later to my dad, John

Herman of Sitka, Alaska. I honestly believe it was more a marriage of necessity than anything else, simply because my mom and dad were constantly drinking. I was told that when I was a few weeks old, Mom just up and left him because of his abusive behavior.

I had tried many times to talk to Mom about my dad, but whenever I brought it up she would just say, "Oh, you don't want to hear about him. He was mean and nothing but a drunk." So I have never bothered her again about my dad.

I even asked my dad's brother, Tony Herman, a few times about him. He would say pretty much the same as Mom. He did say, however, that when my dad was sober, he was just a normal, ordinary person. However, his downfall was booze or liquor of any kind. As soon as he had a few drinks in him he would become mean and angry! To make a long, story short, I have never ever seen a picture of my dad, nor have I ever had anyone tell me any more than what I have written here so I can't say anymore about him.

I was told that he, too, drowned within a year after Mom left him. He had been out fishing in the Sitka area.

I was born on January 15, 1940, in Sitka, Alaska. In April of 1940, my mother moved back to Yakutat with my brother and me to be with her family. It was there that she met and married the only real dad my brother and I ever knew, John Adams.

Lessons of life are learned and taught to us by our loving parents
Love and respect them.

Love Your Parents

The greatest man that I have ever known,
Was the man I called Dad.
I used to think that he could walk on water.
I worshipped him and loved him so.
I never told him enough when he was here.
He left us so suddenly and in the prime of his life.
I miss him and wish I could relive those years.
Of growing up as a family, in God's country.
Children of today, take heed of what I say.
Life is too short to waste it, or throw it all away.
Love your parents and show them you really care.
Tell them so, and hug them whenever you can.
Believe me, I speak from many years of experience.
Our parents are our greatest teachers of life.
Listen, hear and obey your parents while you can.
To talk back while being lectured to was unheard of.
You hung your head and listened obediently when spoken to
And knew it was only because they loved you so.
So, if you have a mother or father, or both,
Jump up out of your chair and tell them you love them.
Hug them and thank them for the lessons you've learned.
Be proud to be a son or daughter of theirs while you can.

3

Dad's Family Tree

Dad used to talk a lot about his early life of growing up in Petersburg.

Dad's father was a full Mexican who came from Old Mexico in the early 1900s. His real name was Juan Adome, but when he came across the border they translated his name as John Adams.

Neither my brother nor I know how he ended up in Petersburg. We believe he came up on a fishing boat to work in the fishing industry. In any event, he met Maggie and they fell in love, and were married.

Maggie was a full-blooded Tlingit, a very religious person who tried to instill those same values in her children. They soon had three sons and a daughter. The eldest was Henry, and then a sister named Alice, then John, and a younger brother named George. Dad was born in 1918 in Petersburg.

When Dad was in his early teens he and his mother had a falling-out of sorts. Because of her strict upbringing, he just couldn't live by her rules. After an attempt to send Dad to school at Wrangell Institute, he managed to get himself expelled because he had not lived by the boarding school rules. He even managed to get accepted to Sheldon Jackson training school. This is where he talked about having a real crush on my mom, but "she wouldn't even give me the time of day," he often said. "She had a long line of suitors waiting by the wayside." Anyway

Dad got booted out of Sheldon Jackson and ended up back in Petersburg. Dad and his mother were still not on speaking terms, so he decided to leave home for good. That was the beginning of what he called his hobo years.

He lived in the woods around Petersburg for a while; picking blueberries and selling them to anyone that would pay for them. He eventually ended up on a seine boat out of Seattle, Washington. After the fishing season ended, he found himself back in Seattle. He told us stories of riding the freight trains all the way to San Francisco, California. This was during the Depression, so he talked of surviving on one bowl of soup and a piece of bread each day from one of the many soup kitchens along the way. Dad somehow ended up in Utah where he managed to find work on a farm with a Mormon family. The experience of living with this Mormon family for over a year taught him the real meaning of family life, and the importance of working hard and sticking together, helping one another.

Dad soon learned how to operate tractors and all. kinds of heavy equipment while in Utah.

After a time, Dad had earned enough money to leave. Upon arriving in Petersburg, he found out that his mother had moved her family to Yakutat, Alaska.

He ended up in Wrangell where he met a girl by the name of Alice. They eventually married and had two daughters named Juanita and Myrna. We don't know why they were divorced, but I believe it was because Dad was such a free-spirited person who loved his alcohol and his freedom.

Alice was a real upstanding lady who wouldn't tolerate that kind of life. I honestly believe it was a mutual kind of understanding to divorce, rather than to cause each other more heartache.

By this time, it seemed that Dad had nowhere else to go, so

he moved to Yakutat, where his family was.

Isn't it amazing after all the time that went by that he would find the love of his life in my mom, his high-school crush? Anyway, they were married in April of 1940 in Yakutat, Alaska. Dad was only five feet seven inches tall, but he had broad shoulders and a real barrel-like chest. He had jet-black hair which he kept combed straight back with a light part right down the middle. He had black eyes and always had a thick, full mustache that was as stiff as a wire brush. Most every winter he would grow a beard that made him look a lot larger than his normal 185-pound frame. He had that rugged Jack Dempsey look, complete with a broken nose, because he used to be a boxer in his younger days. He had a smile that could melt an iceberg, and seemed to light up his eyes, showing his beautiful pearl-white teeth.

Dad used to call Yakutat "God's country" and as we were growing up I learned to appreciate his sensitivity to nature. He used to say "When God made the world he chose Yakutat to be laid out in a way that it would take your breath away."

I have to admit that Yakutat is the only community in the world that can boast several major attractions of record proportions. The second-tallest mountain in North America, rising from sea level to 18,008 feet is Mount Saint Elias. Serving as its foundation is the Malaspina Glacier, which is 850 square miles and, on sunny days, clearly exhibits the fact that it is larger than the state of Rhode Island. Approximately two hundred miles southeast of Mount Saint Elias is Mount Fairweather rising from the Gulf of Alaska 15,300 feet into the heavens; and in between the two mountains lies the Wrangell-Saint Elias Mountain Range.

Yakutat is also the only community in the world that built a railroad exclusively to haul salmon. The ten-mile railroad ran from the downtown cannery to the Situk River, and was used constantly to haul salmon to the cannery up until the mid-1950s.

These are only the beginnings of some of the attractions that we called home—an ideal place in which to grow up; and an ideal place in which to raise children to become responsible adults in the way of learning and to subsist from the bounties of the land; to be self-sufficient in every way.

Memories of the past are all I have left. Always remember, "The way it was is now the way it used to be. Never to return."

Reflections

Memories are but a reflection of one's past experiences.
The good and bad times of life are locked in our brains
Like a bank for deposit or withdrawal, as needed.
Wouldn't it be nice if we could block out the bad times
And only remember the good fun times in our lives?
But we really do need the mix of the good and bad
In order to learn the lessons that life has in store.
Lessons of life are learned through trial and error,
Though some of us will err more than others!
We will all eventually get it right in the end.
Between now and then and between you and me,
I'll continue to reflect on my past experiences to learn
How to cope with the good, the bad and the mediocre times.

4

Mom and Dad's Early Years

Since Dad knew how to operate heavy equipment, he immediately found work as a Cat operator during the war when the airbase was being built in Yakutat, Alaska. In those days this was the third-largest airbase in Alaska and is said to have had up to twenty thousand troops stationed there ready to be shipped to the Pacific at a moment's notice. There were four bunkers of cannons positioned at the entrance of Monti Bay on the banks of Point Carew. There were also huge cannons at what is called Cannon Beach, strategically placed to protect against any invasions from the Japanese.

After the war he was fortunate to be able to go to work for the Civil Aviation Agency before it became the Federal Aviation Agency. He kept the roads maintained by clearing snow in the winter months and graded the gravel roads in the summer. When warranted new roads were built throughout the Yakutat area and he was responsible for keeping them maintained. Bert and I were always very proud and happy to see him whenever he came into town with a piece of heavy equipment. "That's my daaaaad!" Bert and I would holler so everyone within hearing distance could hear us and see him.

Dad was also the town barber, and he even had a barber chair in our house, one that was given to him by the army before they left Yakutat—it was surplus and because he gave haircuts to his army buddies, they had no qualms about letting him have the chair. He stored it in the corner of the living room and pulled it out every Saturday to open up "Johnnie's Barber Shop." He even had a sign that he dusted off every Saturday, and tacked it on the wall that read: 10 CENTS FOR THE HAIRCUT AND 90 CENTS TAX. It was only meant to be humorous, but if he were alive today and could see what we are paying in taxes, he'd be pretty close.

His hair-cutting tools were a set of hand clippers, a comb and a pair of scissors. He used those hand clippers for many years before he broke down and bought himself an electric set. I remember those hand clippers to this day because whenever he cut Bert's and my hair we always regretted that time because those clippers would pull on our hair and by the time we were done with our haircuts we were almost in tears. When he got his electric clippers the vibrations made Bert jump in the chair, especially when Dad was working the right side in back of his head.

"Be still!" Dad would lose patience.

"I can't help it, Dad," Bert would say.

"Why? What's wrong?"

"It tickles right here," and Bert would indicate by pointing his finger at his back on the right side of his rib cage. Invariably, there would be nicks in Bert's head, so Dad would end up cutting his hair short. Because Bert ended up with crew cuts, Dad gave me crew cuts too.

Mom started a bakery, making homemade bread and pies, which were always sold even before they came out of the oven. I can still smell the fresh bread and the different pies like apple, lemon meringue, banana cream, or strawberry/rhubarb when I visualize myself back in our house in Yakutat. She also used to make the best strawberry cream puffs I have ever tasted.

Some of my greatest memories were of the times Dad got off work. My brother and I used to watch for him as he got off the bus, and when either of us spotted him I would go running down the dirt road as fast as I could, hollering "Daddy! Daddy!" He would greet me with his usual facial rubs, rubbing his beard into my face and neck, as I squealed with delight.

His first question was always the same as he handed me his empty lunch box to carry: "Were you good boys today? Did you both do your chores?" as he pretended to box with us. "I'll fight anybody my heavy," he'd say, dancing this way and that way. And then he'd start tickling me right under the rib cage. And then he'd chase after us in his usual Jack Sullivan boxing stance all the way home. Once inside the house he would pick me up and plop me down on the couch and begin wrestling, or tickling me until I had tears in my eyes. Other than his torturous beard rubs to me (he never did this much to Bert—maybe he thought he was too grown for that), he used to take turns on us and first grab me in a headlock, then rub his knuckles back and forth across the top of my head so hard I would be crying and laughing at the same time. After he finished with me he'd catch Bert and do the same to him. These were just some of those special moments with Dad. Even though we knew he was our step-dad he always made us feel like we were something special.

Bert and I had chores to do right after school, so were not allowed to play until after our chores were done and our homework was completed. My job was to take out the garbage, and get a bucket of ice from the ice machine at the dock. Dad always had to have a pitcher of ice-cold water waiting for him when he came home from work. My brother, being three years older than I, had to do all of the heavy work, like packing water, fuel, etc., till I was big enough to help do my share, which came a lot sooner than expected. Our only source of water was piped in from a well to this faucet outside of the local cannery store, where all the local townsfolk had to pack their own water by the bucketful. Before this source of water was made available, people carried their water from streams that ran from lakes into Monti Bay. The water was nice and cold, but people were getting a lot of illnesses that were attributed to the contamination of the water. The new source of water was a blessing to the community and my brother and I capitalized on the demand for water by older people in the village who were not able to carry their own water.

A truth recently realized is hard to swallow, while you confront it as a fact.

My Brother—My Family

Now there is only my brother and me,
Left of a family of four that used to be.
We're both married now with children of our own.
They are our family now and that I've always known.
But, oh, how I wish we could relive those times,
I'd thank Mom and Dad for each and every day,
For the lessons we've learned along the way.
I never told them enough when they were here,
That I love them and thank them for being so dear,
For raising us so our thoughts would be clear
Of the heartache and troubles of those times.
And so, dear brother, I'd sure like to say
Though we are separated each in our own way,
I love you and wish you much happiness in life
And success and freedom from struggles and strife.
Times have changed so much over the years,
The way it was is now the way it used to be
When we lived off the land—in God's country.

5

Being the Town Gopher

Shortly after they married, my dad adopted my brother and me, and we made our home in Yakutat, Alaska. I remember starting first grade when I was just five years old because I always used to follow Bert to school and wouldn't leave when the teacher tried to send me home. I would play with all the other kids until school actually started, then I would entertain myself in the cloakroom until recess time.

I really looked up to my brother, being that he was three years older than me. To me, he was my guardian, my protector, the only one I trusted to protect me from everything. Anyway, the teacher finally said that if I wouldn't go home, I might as well go to school. So I was given a desk behind Bert. She even gave me work to do!

Our school was actually a converted two-story bunkhouse used previously to house many of the Chinese and Filipino cannery workers after the cannery was built in the early 1900s. It was located behind the cannery just above the sandy beach overlooking the beautiful harbor of Monti Bay. I don't remember too much about those early days of schooling, but I sure do remember all the fun we had. It's odd how we remember and can reminisce about the good times.

My brother made an observation one time that he could never remember much about the rainy days when he was a kid. "I can remember," he said, "only the good times, and it always seemed like the days were sunny."

There were actually two different routes to take, or ways for everyone to get to school from the main dirt road. The safe route was to walk along this dirt path directly behind the cannery, which would insure that you'd get to school fairly clean. The other route, and most everyone's choice, was to take this path underneath the cannery, dodging all the creosote pilings, and walking along the sandy beach. This was everyone's favorite route because, as kids, we would always be rubbing up against creosote pilings, or assuring that our shoes were full of sand and wet from dodging the waves on the sandy beach.

It was in 1948 when a new school was built, along with a gymnasium at the other end of the town by the old post office.

I grew up having my share of normal childhood sicknesses, like the mumps, measles and chicken pox, just like most everyone else, but there were also a whole bunch of unusual things that have happened to me as well.

When I was about eight or nine years old I was playing on the rocky beach below our house with my friend Joe Nelson. We used to pride ourselves with our ability to skip rocks along the water. We were always looking for that perfectly rounded and flat rock, a little larger than a silver dollar, that fit just right in between your thumb and forefinger.

I was standing about ten feet away from my friend, to his right, just watching him begin his wind-up to skip his rock that he said would be the world record. As he reared back and began his forward swing, he slipped on some kelp and barnacles. I suddenly felt like I had been hit with a sledgehammer.

The rock he threw was now embedded in my forehead, just above my right eyebrow. I fell to my knees thinking I was dying! Reaching up to feel the cut, the rock came loose and dropped to the ground. I began to think I would to bleed to death.

My friend immediately sprang into action, tearing his shirtsleeve off, and applied it directly to my forehead and told me to hold it tightly! This calmed me down enough to where he could finally escort me up the embankment and to my house.

I was taken out to the army base where the medic put eight stitches in my forehead to close the cut. I stayed home nursing a headache for the rest of the day, but was right back to playing on the beach again the following day, proudly showing off the bandaged forehead to my friends.

This next incident happened to me the following year in April, while looking around near the cannery area for some clean ice because the ice machine on the front of the dock had broken down.

With bucket in hand I was tromping around the cannery area looking for solid pieces of ice instead of snow. I was just bent over by this shed when I suddenly stood up and walked right into a nail that was sticking out of the 2″x 4″ that stuck out of the rafter of the shed. This nail "scrape" caused a two-inch gash just about my left eyebrow that required four stitches.

I became quite safety conscious for a while, I guess, because nothing much happened to me for the next few years.

In the early spring many of the residents would congregate on the dock using hand lines to jig for small halibut, herring, or smelt. I was always down on the dock myself, trying to catch that "big" one. I never did catch anything except a few bullheads and some small flounders. I believe my sophisticated equipment was just too much for those large halibut to handle.

I normally used hanging twine with either a rock or a piece of pipe tied to the end for weight. About two feet above my weight I tied a short line with the largest treble hook I could find. My bait usually consisted of a chunk of the foulest smelling piece of bullhead or rotten herring!

In order to get my hook out far enough away from the dock, I usually had to twirl my line over my head like a lasso and throw as hard as I could. This one day I was twirling my line when my weight came off, causing a kind of backlash action. This caused my hook to embed itself into my left middle finger with the point just protruding out of the center of my fingernail!

I was certainly lucky because the barbed part of the hook didn't penetrate my finger. Someone just grabbed the hook and pulled it out of my fingernail, and sent me home to bandage it up. Well, needless to say, I lived to fish another day!

We also had to pack our own fuel oil for the cookstove and an oil heater which we used in the winter months in the upstairs area of our house.

I felt like I became everyone's errand boy, or the town's gopher, always doing something for the less fortunate elderly people of Yakutat. My brother had a clientele as well, and even though we may have been competitors, we didn't seem to compete with one another for business. The demand was there for anyone to take, and he worked his trade and I mine, only sharing who had made the most money in the day. Bert's first priority was to split and stack firewood for our grandmother, Minnie Johnson. I did the water carrying. Those of you who have grown up in a small community would understand what I mean because every small community seems to have someone like me around.

I had a little red wagon Dad had to buy me because I was turning away work, simply because I was still too small to carry more than half a bucket of water at a time. It soon became apparent to me that I needed to have softer tires on my wagon because of the graveled roads, and the steep hill I had to traverse while doing my errands. Dad replaced the hard rubber tires with soft, air-filled airplane tail-wheel tires, that had just enough air in each tire to make the roughest road seem like a smooth asphalt road. Dad said it was an old Indian trick or something, but I was so proud of my little red wagon I felt like I owned a dump truck. As soon as I'd finished my chores after school, I was off hauling either a sack of coal, two buckets of water, or fuel oil for someone almost daily. This meant that most of the weekdays I was kept busy, and didn't have much time to play after supper like the other children.

However, I would make up for the lost time on the weekends because it seemed like I was always getting into some kind of mischief. If I wasn't playing marbles with my friends, then I was either down on the beach breaking bottles, under the dock climbing around, or I'd be out exploring somewhere.

We used to take great pride making our weapons of destruction, mainly slingshots. There must have been at least six of us boys that used to pal around together, and in the early spring we'd spend hours searching among alders looking for that perfect Y for our slingshots. We used old inner tubes, cut in strips so they stretched just right, and used the leather tongues of old shoes for the pebble holder.

We actually used to have contests on the rocky beach below our house, where we would set up a bunch of glass bottles spaced a certain length apart in a straight line on the rocks. Each one of us would get ten shots at ten bottles. Whoever would break the most bottles would win a candy bar, or a cookie, or whatever we had at the time. Of course, if I wasn't shooting at or breaking bottles, then we'd be climbing around under the dock, chasing ducks, loons, or seagulls.

We'd have our pockets full of pebbles from the beach to use for our ammo supply, so we'd be weighted down pretty good as we climbed around this fish trough that ran from the main cannery to the end of the dock. This trough was used to dump all the fish scraps, etc. from the cannery. If we happened to be wading in the trough, and didn't hear this gush of water every once in awhile, we'd get caught and be standing in about a foot of water, all mixed with fish scraps, tails, heads, and it would be soon slippery and grimy.

Another one of our favorite games was exploring, or combing new territory. There were many cannery bunkhouses around the area of the cannery that were now vacant and all boarded up with plywood on the windows and doors. This didn't stop us kids from finding ways of getting into those old buildings and literally tearing them apart from the inside out.

This was where we could spend our time when the weather was bad, playing our war games, or whatever. We would literally tear the plywood off the wall and build forts where we would pretend we were camping out in the wilderness. A couple of times we almost burned one of those buildings down, because we'd build a campfire that would get out of hand. Somehow we managed to always douse the campfire before the whole place went up in flames.

On weekends, during the winter months, when the weather was too nasty for us boys to play outside, Mom used to let me invite a few of my friends to stay overnight. I had a large collection of comic books that my friends and I used to trade. My favorite ones were Archie and Jughead and Superman.

We used to sit around reading comic books or telling each other scary stories till it was time to go to bed. Mom would make a pot of hot chocolate and we'd have a piece of homemade apple pie before we'd stretch out on the floor in our sleeping bags to go to sleep.

I used to pride myself on being a pretty darn good cook because I used to watch my mother around the stove all the time, and one of my favorite sweets was chocolate fudge. Now I must tell you when you're a kid, anything that is sweet probably tastes pretty good, no matter what it's supposed to be. My first few batches of fudge were, of course, a disaster because when I watched Mom do it, she never measured her ingredients. Well, I would begin by dumping some sugar in a pot, and pouring in some canned milk, then pouring in a whole can of cocoa and mixing it all together, thinking it would soon turn thick and when cooled, would be nice chewy fudge just like Mom always made. It never turned out. though, always ending up like tar. We loved to spoon this mess out of the pot anyway; as long as it was sweet it was good to us.

Dad was very swift with his discipline of my brother and me. I must have been quite the mischievous rascal because I remember many a time when I got a good spanking. Dad raised us boys to obey his rules or pay the consequences. The rules were simple enough: come directly home after school, do our daily chores, and no playing outside unless our homework was done. If we didn't have a legitimate excuse for not doing our chores, we would get a good spanking and that was always understandable to us boys; even though we didn't always agree with this philosophy, we at least understood.

He would always explain why we needed the spanking if we were to get one, usually just before he spanked us. Then usually about a half hour afterwards, he'd come to us in our bedroom and make peace. Like I said before, he was making us understand right from wrong and enforcing his rule of punishment, then love and affection after the punishment.

The sounds, the smells, and even the feelings may be gone, but they are certainly not forgotten.

Gone, But Not Forgotten

I miss the rhythmic sound of coffee
perking on an old wood stove,
And the crackling sound of wood burning itself to ashes,
The smell of coffee and pancakes wafting through our cabin,
The many sounds of different birds
singing by my window at sunrise,
And even the pitter-patter sound of raindrops on the tin roof,
The warm feeling of the first rays of morning
sunshine on my face,
I even miss the goose bumps I got when listening
to a coyote howl,
Or the snorting sound of a bull moose
as it caught my scent in the wind.
I really miss the chattering sound
of my pet squirrels nibbling at my feet,
Or the screeching sound of a bald eagle as it catches a salmon,
And the constant soothing roar of the ocean waves
splashing to shore.
Yes, I even miss the constant backaches
from picking salmon out of my net,
And the stiff joints in my fingers and wrists
from being cold and wet all the time.
The miraculous healing when I got my settlement
money each fall,
I even miss the long, boring winter months
of waiting to do it all over again.
If I had but one wish in my lifetime that would come true,
I'd wish, without hesitation, to relive my growing years again
With my family, when we lived off the land—in God's country.

6

Yakutat—The Village

I believe that the Yakutat area is truly the crown jewel of Alaska. With over one hundred miles of gray crystalline sand along the coastline stretching from Ocean Cape to Litulia Bay is magnificent construction by the Creator; and there is the beautiful blue-green Pacific Ocean waves forever frothing, and churning as they deposit their salty, foamy bubbles onto the grainy beach; and then the ever-present roar of the surf, soothing to troubled senses, is indeed comforting; a combination of any of these can awaken the soul so that it transmits you to oblivion and even snatches your subconscious away from the cares and concerns of everyday events.

In those days the salmon were plentiful in the rivers and streams and their tributaries, through what is known as the Yakutat Forelands. The Forelands extends from Yakutat all the way to Litulia Bay, and is one huge spawning bed for the various species of salmon, not only in Alaska, but nationwide. This was why so many people of various nationalities had begun to migrate to the small communities (particularly to Southeast Alaska) to work in the canneries, or to try their luck at commercial fishing.

There were two general stores in the village. The major one was the store owned by Libby McNeil and Libby, who also owned the cannery. The other was Mallott's General Store, which was begun by J.B. Mallott, who served as Yakutat's mayor for many years.

It seemed that prices were staggering, simply. because most food items had to be freighted from the south forty-eight. Alaska Steamship Company transported merchandise from Seattle; they would make a trip about every three months, so it was always quite a treat when we saw the huge vessel emerge around Ankow Point, enter Yakutat Bay, and then turn into Monti Bay where the community of Yakutat was perched along the hillside. I remember the excitement the sighting caused among us kids, who would run up and down the thoroughfare and holler, like the town crier, "The steamer is coming! The steamer is coming!" This always incited in us the prospects of replenishing dwindling supplies and discovering new inventions.

Since fishing was the predominant livelihood, most everyone in the community would move to their respective fishing camps for the summer. About ninety percent of the population fished in the Situk and Ahrnklin Rivers along the coastline of Yakutat, located about ten miles from town, heading southeast.

Since fishing for a livelihood proved to be a gamble among our people, it was the only major game in town, so most everyone took part in the gamble of life in this small fishing village.

The first two years we fished and lived on the Alsek River and then the next ten years on the Akwe River. This was our birthright country, and where we actually grew up to be men.

In those days of transition most everyone would have to open charge accounts at the two stores during the winter, and spend the summer trying to earn enough money to pay off their winter's debt. It was a constant cycle, and my parents were no different than most members of the community.

But things could have been different and more prosperous if they did not drink, or had used their resources more wisely. I think things would have been more prosperous for us if alcohol had not become so important to them because they were both well educated.

Dad did not finish high school, but he was well read and had a vision that was remarkable for those day's standards. As I look back on our people's history, I find that they were a remarkable breed and probably their biggest downfall was alcohol. It proved to be so with my mother, our stepdad, and many good people from Yakutat. It would also prove to be the demise of me, my own family, as well as my brother, Bert. Not only did our generation lose our language and our culture, we lost our dignity and identity as well. What a tragedy this has been.

Our father was a patriot, and even though he did not serve in the armed services during the war when all his buddies did, he worked for the army corp of engineers as a heavy equipment operator. When the airport at Yakutat was being built, he was what is called a "Cat skinner" and bulldozed the foundation trench for the airport. The ground in which he worked was swamp and muskeg, and he was given the nickname Muskeg because that was where they had always seen him from the beginning of work until the day's end. The Yakutat airport became the third largest airfield in Alaska and camped about twenty thousand troops. No doubt it had become a very strategic place during the war. At the entrance of Monti Bay, on Point Carew, there were four bunkers, accommodating large cannons which would be used to protect the harbor in case of an invasion. There were also cannons along the beach about five or six miles from Point Carew, which is now called Cannon Beach. There isn't much evidence of the army base left now because it was all cleaned up over the years; all there is now are the cannons and the two runways that the commercial airlines use.

In any event, my father was one person I learned to admire because of his ability to learn well whatever it was he was engaged in. When my brother and I became old enough he began to teach us the tricks of the trade in the commercial set net industry—first on the Alsek River and then later on the Akwe River.

He was well read, and loved to read good books and meaningful articles in magazines. His favorite author was Mickey Spillane. As for our mother, she was a jewel. Whenever we needed comfort from a minor cut or injury, whether the injury be a physical bruise or hurt feelings, we could always count on her to help soothe pain. She graduated from high school and on the very same afternoon eloped with my brother's dad. She wanted to be a doctor—probably the first Native and woman doctor in Alaska. She won scholarships and was accepted to attend Gonzaga University in Washington, where she would take nurse's training, and then eventually go to medical school. However, Bert was the reason she had to give up her medical plans. He was born just when she was making plans to go to college in Washington. She never did make it to fulfill her dream.

As a child, we will deny ever becoming a parent. We pray for continued life and health and we love our parents so.

Parents

Most of us will become parents within our lifetime
As a child, we will deny it with a squeaky voice
But as we grow up and mature, it's a matter of choice
We fall in love, and soon have children of our own
We nurture them through feeding schedules and moan and groan
Through sleepless nights of colic and teething pains
Of diaper changes and washing out the dirty stains
Somehow we prevail, though I don't know how
Our parents are so special; we call them Mom and Pop now
They're in their bonus years of life now, and we love them so
These simple words I write are to let them know
We seek their wisdom and guidance each and every day
Their faith in God keeps them going, come what may
That same love of God is imbedded deep in our mind
It is utmost in our thoughts so we can find
Peace and contentment in our daily living
We thank you for your sharing and for giving
We know in our hearts you have done your best
To share your thoughts on life freely and all the rest
So, Mom and Pop, we all just want you to know.

7

Living with Our Paternal Grandmother

There was a period of time one summer when Bert and I stayed with our paternal grandmother, Maggie Adams, and sixteen of our cousins in her large two-story house; that summer our parents were fishing in the Alsek River and because they were just getting started couldn't take us with them.

Grandmother's house was located in the older part of Yakutat; we called it the "old village." I remember well the Tlingit design panels and murals that decorated the entire ceiling and one wall of the living room. Her house was a traditional tribal house, and was probably one of the last surviving ones in the old village.

The main gravel road annexing the town with the village ran right in front of the house; below the road was a beautiful sandy beach; here we could hear the ever-present sound of the ocean waves echoing to the community from the formidable Pacific Ocean.

All of us children bunked upstairs with one section cordoned off by drapes that hung from the ceiling. The drapes separated the sections where the boys and girls slept.

As mentioned earlier, there was my brother, Bert, and L along with cousins David, Daniel, Barbara, and Henry Phillips. Both parents of these kids were no longer living and Grandma took them and raised them. And then there was Henry, Matthew, Margaret, Mary, Clifford, Harlan, Situk, Stanley and Peter

Adams. Their parents were Dad's older brother, Henry, and his wife, May. Uncle Henry fished on the Alsek River that year with my dad; May originally came from Kake, and moved with her husband to Yakutat. And then there were Alice's children, Walter, Theresa, Henry, Albert, and Nellie Porter. Grandma was a widow and I really don't know how, or why, all of us kids came to stay with her but I believe our parents were fishing out in the Alsek River or Dry Bay.

Grandma was a very religious woman and had an altar set up alongside her bed, where she would sometimes spend hours in prayer. Grandma could speak English quite well, though her words didn't quite fit together if she became excited or angry. In the privacy of her home she preferred to speak the Tlingit language, especially when praying or when disciplining us children.

I remember many times us kids would still be up talking and giggling after we were sent to bed at nine o'clock. Grandma would holler at us from downstairs, using a few choice Tlingit phrases we all understood, but when she was really upset she would use her very worst English phrase: "What the heck— what's the matter for you kids anyway?" When she said that, we all knew she was really angry and we settled down right away.

It was during this time spent with Grandma that I learned to love eating traditional Native foods, such as seal meat and seal oil, which we called grease, because we used it in place of butter. I acquired a taste for Indian candy, which was seal blubber cut into cubes and fried until crispy. That summer we moved to the Situk River where she fished and planted a huge garden that she had us all work on. I remember the large carrots and turnips, rutabagas, potatoes, and other stuff that we harvested in midsummer and fall. It was fun to sneak into the garden when the carrots and turnips were ready. One of my cousins, Harlan, loved turnips and was given that nickname. To this day, only those of us who knew his nickname at that time still called him that. He and

Clifford were twins, and it seemed that Clifford was always ill from something because of those cold:-water baths, but he was given the nickname "Sick Boy."

Harlan and Clifford were about my age, maybe a little younger, but we became close playmates. Bert and Matthew were the same age, and Situk was younger and close by a year, so they all hung around together. They played more grown-up stuff than we did; while we played with makeshift toys in the sand, they liked to play with their handmade boats in the river.

I noticed quite often that when the others got tired of playing boats, that Bert would always continue playing by himself. He was quite a craftsman, using whatever he could find to make his toys. I think his favorite was taking an old cedar wooden cork he'd found on the beach and split it in half. With one piece he would make a sailboat and cut a small piece of the cover of a tin can and insert it on the rear to serve as a rudder. Then he would follow it along the shore as it bobbed and sailed under the force of the westerly winds. With the other half of the cork he would make wings and tails and fashion amphibious airplanes. My brother, Bert, was very creative.

Grandma did her best to raise us in the traditional Tlingit way, bless her heart, she meant well, but I guess didn't realize that at times she seriously put some of our lives in jeopardy.

First, I think I need to explain that our ancestors used to turn their boys over to someone else to raise and teach about history, culture, songs and dances, etc. This kind of intellectual cultivation was reserved for the elders in the community, like a grandfather or some respected person who had gained stature and wisdom through storytelling. When a boy became seven years old he was rotated to his uncle, the uncle, in time, would begin to teach the youngster about hunting, fishing and survival. One of the ways they used to toughen the boys was to have them bathe in cold sea water every day. The dipping would not be very long, but long enough to get a chill through the body. This was a tradition that was practiced every day spring, summer, fall and winter. After the bath, the uncle would then slap the youngster with a willow stick to help get the blood circulating through the body. This ritual was designed to help the boy grow fast and become strong and able to endure the toughest of the hardships that would be challenges in the future.

Well, our grandmother was a traditionalist in every way, and every morning at six o'clock, without fail, she would march us boys down to the beach, wearing nothing but our shorts, and rain or shine we were made to wade into the freezing water up to our waists and dunk ourselves under; as we came out of the water shivering and sometimes crying from the cold, Grandma would be waiting with an alder branch, ready to lightly slap our bodies to increase the blood circulation. I don't think she realized that our circulation was stimulated just fine from dancing around and trying to avoid being slapped with that alder branch. No matter what we did, though, she managed to stimulate us all before we were marched back up to the house.

I'm not sure if it was from those early morning baptisms or what, but many of us got sick, sometimes for weeks on end, with colds or the flu. Many of us missed a lot of school because of sickness and I believe the school principal finally notified Dad about the ritual ocean dunking, believing that was the reason we were always sick.

Dad apparently contacted Grandma to stop the ritual, who insisted she was only trying to make us strong. However, the early morning baths soon ended. The next summer, Bert and I were taken to Dry Bay, and from that time forth we spent the rest of the summers in the Dry Bay area, either fishing on the Alsek River or later on the Akwe River.

Knowing how it was, and realizing that was the way it used to be, is hard to leave behind.

Feelings

My coffee is cold and I'm feeling so old,
Just sitting here thinking about days past.
I know I should have left here a long time ago,
But, you know, I can't even bear the thought
Of leaving this old familiar place.
This old cabin means everything to me,
I helped build it way back in '58.
It's not much really, but it's all I have left,
And the memories of the good times we had.
Both Mom and Dad are gone now.
I guess it's time to leave this place and the memories behind.
Before I close the door, I take one last look around
And say a silent prayer of thanks for the good times.
As I walk to the sandy bank, my pet squirrels are chattering.
They know I am saying goodbye, as I throw them one last snack
Of bacon rind. And as I look back, I can see the
Tears in their eyes, too, as I walk down the trail.

8

Subsistence Versus Commercial Fishing

Sometime after the first part of October, Mom and Dad had returned, and soon my brother and I moved back into our house up town. The transition from the subsistence lifestyle to that of commercial fishing was a gradual transition for our people.

In the early 1900s, a cannery was built near the head of Monti Bay. This modernization gradually ushered in the quest for money.

There were some people who still had respect for tradition and some who had vessels that would travel from river to river in the Yakutat area from Icy Bay to Dry Bay.

Hanging our nets for the upcoming fishing season was always a happy time for everyone. It was a time when whole families would get together to help each other, making certain everyone had their nets ready for the opening day of the season. All of the younger children would be given the task of threading the hanging needles with hanging twine, used to attach the web onto the lead line and cork line. They would also have to thread the corks or floats onto the cork line, making certain there were enough floats on the line, depending on what species of salmon you were fishing for. For example, the king salmon or Chinook, is the largest salmon species; therefore the mesh size of the web is larger than either the sockeye or silver salmon web. You also had to have more floats or corks spaced closer together because of the heavier weight. If you didn't have enough floats, your whole net would sink out of sight.

Once you'd hung your cork line on to your web, the only other thing needed was a long buoy line of about five or six fathoms with a large float at the end with your name and fishing license number on it in large bold letters. With an anchor attached at each end of the anchor line, you now had a complete net ready to set, wherever your heart desired.

The Alsek or Dry Bay is the only river in the Yakutat area that has a king salmon fishery. Although the king salmon do migrate into most of the other rivers, they do so sporadically and their numbers are sparse. For instance, the Situk River is well known for steelhead and king and silver salmon sport-fishing seasons. I mean, you are allowed to fish during the openings, but only with a rod and reel.

The openings for each of the three different species of salmon vary from year to year depending on the migrating cycle of each species. In those days the king salmon season in the Alsek River began around the first of May to about the first of June to mid-July to about the first of August, when the silver or coho salmon started their annual migration. They normally ran all the way up to the end of September or early October.

The next summer, Bert and I were taken to Dry Bay, and from that time forth we spent the rest of the summers in the Dry Bay area either fishing on the Alsek River or later on the Akwe River.

During the off-fishing season Dad was lucky to be working for the Civil Aviation Agency as a heavy equipment operator, but as time went by it seemed like my parents began to drink more and more. Though our daily life was normal and routine, I know now that my parents were true alcoholics. Even though they would drink a lot they never ever neglected my brother and me, and we always had food in the house to eat.

I wasn't aware at the time, but many of our Native people

were serving their country during the war. Some of the ones that did serve were now back in the village living with their families and raising families of their own. All of a sudden the town had a whole new generation of young adults in their early twenties with a whole lot of energy. Alcohol and its related problems became the major concern in the community and were literally tearing families apart.

In the 1950s the fish cannery, owned by Libby McNeil and Libby, sold to Bellingham Canning Co. The new owners immediately began to upgrade their processing capabilities. One of the things they did was eliminate the canning portion and added a large fast-freeze storage facility, which enhanced their product and, thereby, the demand for fresh-caught salmon brought a better price. These changes made it more lucrative for the fishermen, who now stood a better chance to prosper in the fishing business.

Bellingham Canning Co. was also more willing to outfit groups of fishermen, mainly large families, into small companies, and each person received a full share of the profits.

The Army and Navy had plenty of surplus equipment such as dump trucks, Jeeps, and many small boats or large landing crafts. Many of these trucks and boats had been purchased by the new owners of the cannery and leased or sold directly to a few of the fishermen.

There seemed to be a new area of fishing for the people of Yakutat, mainly this territory near Icy Bay—practically right alongside Mt. Saint Elias. This moved away from the more popular fishing areas like the Situk and Ahrnklin Rivers, and the Dry Bay region, for the more newly founded fishing area of the Icy Bay area.

These new fishing ventures took the pressure off from the real crowded areas and made it possible for most all of the people of Yakutat to renew ties with their ancestral homelands.

True friends will always be there for you if they are true, indeed.

Friends

True friends will never ever forsake you
They will always be there for you in time of need.
Have you ever tried to quit a bad habit
Like drinking or maybe smoking cigarettes?
You thought all your friends would support you,
But instead, those so-called friends tried
To keep you from quitting in order to support their habit.
Over time you will prevail and know who your real friends are.
The ones who support you are still by your side,
While the ones you supported while drinking are gone.
Therein lies the difference between all so-called friends.

9

Quality Control

In the fifties and sixties there really wasn't much in the way of entertainment other than the weekly movies at the Alaska Native Brotherhood Hall. The pool hall was open on weekends for adults only, because they used to gamble in the back card room.

It was during these early years that I first got introduced to alcohol on a personal basis. Dad would bootleg cases of whiskey that he had bought from a liquor store and flown in from Juneau. Not much profit was realized from this venture, as most of the stock was consumed by my parents and their friends before it had a chance to be sold. Whenever whiskey didn't arrive or get ordered, Dad would make a batch of home brew. I became quite adept at siphoning it from the barrel into the bottles. Bert would put the caps on them. Mom would supervise us, of course. I couldn't siphon a bottle without tasting it first. As I look back on it now, I guess I regarded myself as the quality control person. Quality control had certain drawbacks, however, such as falling right to sleep after bottling each batch.

Whenever there was whiskey to sell I would have to service the customers that would show up at two or three in the morning because Mom or Dad would be somewhere else or asleep.

I remember my first sale well because my customer was one of the old-timers, William Thomas. He couldn't speak English well and he pronounced my name "Cop-eye."

We were awakened to the desperate pounding on our door

early one morning. I opened the door and there he was, a short old man, knees bent, glasses hanging on the end of his nose, shaking from too many years of drink. It took a while for him to recognize me and even longer for me to understand what he wanted. He smiled at me and asked, "Cop-eye, can you open my eye just a niddle bit?"

I stood there in the doorway unable to understand him until he put his thumb to his mouth and tipped his head back as if he were drinking from a bottle. When I caught onto what he wanted, I told him to wait while I checked Dad's stash in the cupboard by the stairs. I came back with two bottles of beer and handed them to him. It seemed that he couldn't thank me enough. He backed out of the door and into the night repeating. "Tank you, Cop-eye. You saved my life. Tank you."

When Mom and Dad would drink, they would have two or three other couples over, so my brother and I learned how to entertain ourselves the best we could during these times. We would go upstairs and play with our toys—Bert was always working on a model airplane, or drawing pictures, or doing something creative. Downstairs we could hear all that was going on. Dad would bring out his guitar and he and Mom and their friends would all sing songs. I remember many nights waking up to tunes like, "You Are My Sunshine," "Mockingbird Hill," or "Four Walls." Sometimes they would start a certain song and someone would say, "That's too sad," and they'd start another one.

Now Dad's idea of good entertainment was to put boxing gloves on my brother and me and watch us pound each other silly. Dad would be so proud of us boys, telling his friends that he was making men out of us. My brother, being three years older than I, had to kneel down and I'd be standing up, with boxing gloves that I could barely lift. We would begin to pound on each other until either my nose bled too much, or my brother would just quit because he'd feel sorry for me, all the while Dad and his friends would be cheering us on. Bert, to this day, always credits those bouts to his being able to defend himself well in real fights in his younger days because he had to stay on his knees when we boxed. "It was during those bouts that I learned to move on my knees to keep away from you," he said. "And then when I got into real fights it was easier to move around normally, and also protect my face with my fists because I got the practice and know-how from trying to keep you from hitting me."

Whenever they would drink, Dad would have a bad hangover the next day, and Mom would have to wait on him, bringing him ice water and soup, or whatever. I remember this one weekend when both of them slept 'til late in the afternoon. Bert and I were up and had opened up a can of soup for ourselves when Dad hollered down to me to bring him a sandwich and a glass of ice water. I opened up this can I thought was corned beef hash and made a couple of sandwiches and took them up to Dad along with a glass of ice water. Later that afternoon, Mom told me that Dad really liked the sandwiches I made, but wondered what I used because she didn't have any kind of sandwich spread. I told her I used the corned beef that was in the cupboard. She looked puzzled as she looked in the cupboard and just smiled when she saw the label. It was a can of dog food!

One time Mom had to buy bread from the local store because the store ran out of flour so she couldn't bake her own bread. As she opened the loaf of bread, it was all green and moldy, and she told Dad to take it back and get another one. Dad proceeded to the store, all the while getting madder and madder, saying to himself, "They expect us to pay for moldy bread, do they?" As he entered the store, he threw the bread onto the counter and walked over to the store window which happened to be directly over the beach area. Dad opened the window and began tossing out all the bread from the shelf. He must have thrown out two or three dozen loaves of bread! He, no doubt, had a real Mexican temper that would make one sit up and take notice. Believe me, that was how Dad was, and no one, not even Milt Bristol, who was the bookkeeper and manager of the store, said a single word to him. Afterwards, Bristol told my mother when she went to the store to apologize on behalf of Dad, "Everyone has their own way of expressing themselves. This is one way that John can show his dissatisfaction about our services here at the store."

Another comment was made by Bob Welch, the son of the owner of Bellingham Canning Company. "That combination of Mexican and Indian!" he said, "When he gets mad, his temper is enough to make an Irishman run."

Yet Dad had a charm, when he was inclined to, that was perfectly designed in his personality to charm even an angry bear into submission. An example is when he would get Mom mad and he would leave home for hours at a time. Normally he'd stay at the pool hall until it closed at one or two in the morning. When he decided to come home, he would tiptoe up the stairs to the door, then he'd open the door a crack and say, "Hello, Missy," throwing his hat inside the house. If the hat came flying back out, he'd go out and party some more. Ordinarily, she would be calmed enough the next time he tried the hat trick; when it didn't come flying out the door, he'd edge his way inside.

"Hello missy," he'd say. "I'm sorry, missy."

His hat would be lying on the floor, and he'd pick it up, and with hat in hands, he'd beg her forgiveness for whatever it was he had made her so angry with him about. Things were back to normal for a while—that was until the next time.

More often than not, Mom would join Dad in his drinking episodes, and when they both were engaged, things got unorganized for us. Again, Bert became the father and mother in our lives. It was he that I looked up to in my earlier years; I depended on him to make sure that I was well taken care of. One of the comments I heard him make so many times was that "No matter what, I am never, never, going to drink." I, too, felt that way and we vowed to one another that we would never let this addiction take over our lives—at least that's the way it would be for him.

So many things happened right after the war ended, and being quite young at the time I don't remember too many of the major events that changed a lot of people's lives in Yakutat.

Mom's dad, Charlie, had built a large house right in the center of town. He had married a widow by the name of Minnie Gray. They had a small convenience store set up in the front part of their home where they sold pop and candy, and many baked goods. Grandma Minnie was well known for her fresh baked bread, as well as for making Indian moccasins, which she also displayed and sold.

They also had a fish camp way up the Ahrnklin River. It was exciting when we would go out to their camp in the early spring to watch them catch their salmon and seal, and harvest seaweed and berries which they would put up for the long winter's food supply.

In 1945, right after the war ended, Charlie was diagnosed with cancer of the stomach. He was given just six months to live.

He and Dad became quite close friends, especially after Mom and Dad first got married. It was probably because Dad had a lot of booze available in those days and Charlie would always come by the house saying he was just checking on the welfare of his favorite daughter. Dad would of course invite him to share a few drinks with him, and sometimes he wouldn't leave until the booze was all gone.

When Mom and Dad got married, we lived in a small two-story house that was built on the hill above the store, dock, and cannery. A trail—almost a road—came from the main dirt road in front of the house, and then leveled off for a hundred yards or so, and then there was another steep up-climb.

One wet and icy day in December, Charlie came for a visit and he and Dad got into some home brew. When Charlie decided to go home, Dad decided to help Charlie because the road was very slippery and wet. Mom cautioned them to be careful, and Dad assured her that he would make sure her dad got home safely. Twenty minutes later they were back, Charlie helping my dad into the door. They were both soaking wet, but Dad was quite drunk and too tired to stand, so he fell right into bed and fell asleep.

Charlie said he had to help Dad back because, as they got over the hill and were starting down this steep incline, Dad had fallen down and slid to the bottom of this hill. He tried to get up, but had fallen down three times. Charlie had left Dad and made it home okay, but Dad could never live this experience down. For a long time afterward at gatherings, Mom would always bring this story up saying, "Remember that time when you were supposed to have helped Dad home?"

Charlie actually lived for more than a year, although he suffered terribly near the end. I remember many nights when Mom and Dad would spend hours at her dad's place, taking their turn sitting with him and offering comfort as best as they could. He finally passed away in December of 1947.

True concern and caring can be rewarded with a very wonderful song.

Fly South Young Bird

I nursed a sick bird in my back yard all winter long
It didn't fly south with the rest of his throng
It made no sound at all, not even a whistle
As it appeared to feed daily, from the thorns and thistle
Many times I thought it had died, and was no longer there
But through pouring rain, snow, blizzards, and bitter cold
I would watch that young bird, slowing growing old
It wouldn't, or couldn't fly, though I never saw it try
As it hopped on the ground, coming from a tree limb nearby.
Finally one day in May, just out of the blue
I watched this young bird, as it finally flew
Up to the tallest treetop, as I called out to my wife
To witness this moment, this great event in our life
It fluttered, and danced, and sang a beautiful song
Of Thanksgiving for nursing him all winter long
Then, as if on cue, it flew off into the clear blue sky
I smiled, cause I knew it was finally saying goodbye.

10

Combating Cabin Fever

The Christmas season was by far the best time of the year for most every folk in the community. I know it was for my brother and me. It was always the subject of much talk among us kids in school and while we were playing. The Presbyterian Church would have their choir caroling around town a few nights before Christmas. Mom and Dad joined the choir, which was conducted by Dave Karsten, the school principal and teacher. When this began to take place, the entire town came alive to prepare and help in some way for the traditional Christmas Eve gathering which was always held at the Alaska Native Brotherhood Hall.

In November the school would begin practicing a play, and I remember my brother participating. One year he played the part of the ghost of Christmas Past in the play *A Christmas Carol*. His best buddy, Ted Valle, played the very difficult part of Scrooge, and did an outstanding job of acting.

The hall would be decorated and a large Christmas tree would be set up in the corner with lights and all the ornaments, where everyone would bring their presents to place under the tree to be distributed by Santa's helpers.

I will never forget the times when the master of ceremonies would interrupt the school play to inform the audience the Federal Aviation Agency had picked up some strange lights on their radar, headed in our direction. Us kids would "oh" and "ah" when these announcements were made, knowing Santa was on his way. Then we would try and concentrate on finishing the play or reciting our parts. Some of us had a hard time remembering our lines, but we managed to stumble through to the end and bow, and the girls curtsied, to the applause of our parents, families and friends. At the end of the program someone would announce that bright lights were just spotted over the cannery.

A few minutes later, all us kids would let out a shriek, as we heard the familiar bell; Santa Claus entered the front door, shouting his famous, "Ho! Ho! Ho!" We would gather around as he made his way to the front row of chairs to pass out candy canes, and we looked into his eyes and some of us kids were brave enough to tug at his beard to try to guess who was playing Santa.

Santa would then produce a list of adult names that he would call upon to help begin passing out all the presents from under the tree. As soon as Santa would name off his helpers, they would announce to everyone "please stay seated" until the presents were distributed.

The Alaska Native Brotherhood and Sisterhood officials knew pretty well beforehand which families couldn't afford much of anything for their children, so they always had a bunch of presents stashed away in the back room so that no one ever got left out. Every family also received a box of fruits, hard candies and nuts, etc., so it was always a great time for everyone.

Winter sports were something we always looked forward to with anticipation. We did a lot of sledding. Many of us made our own wooden sleds, and used metal strapping for the runners. Other items used for sliding were old conveyer belts made of rubber from the cannery. We'd cut two- or three-foot sections and use them like toboggans. The ultimate toboggan though was a good sheet of tin, flattened out of its grooves, or curls, and curved up at the front. Sometimes there would be as many as ten kids on a sheet of tin, all shrieking to our hearts' content as we came down our favorite hill we called "Suicide Hill." It was called "Suicide Hill" because it was so narrow and steep, and had a sharp curve near the end, as it flattened out to the entrance of the dock.

I think another reason it was called Suicide Hill was because of what happened to Bert one time. It was when the school was at the Chinese Bunkhouse. Kids were sliding down the hill when he was on his way to school. He walked across the road at the bottom of the hill, and lo and behold, his cousin Daniel Phillips and a friend, Jimmy Jack, were coming down the hill. The sled was a store-bought manufactured one and moved at lightning speed. Daniel had put a blazo box on the sled and sat on top of the box, holding onto the rope that connected to the steering columns. He was pretending that he was on a stagecoach. Jimmy Jack was riding shotgun sitting behind him. It was a dark, dreary afternoon, and it was hard to see because of the shadows from the trees alongside the road and the cannery buildings on the other side of the road. As Bert was crossing the bottom of the road, Daniel's sled was just approaching. Neither saw the other. There was a loud thud, and then screams and bodies tumbling all along the road. Kids ran to the scene, expecting that someone was dead. After bodies stopped sliding and tumbling, Daniel and Jimmy got up and shook the snow off their clothes. Bert lay still, face down in the snow. Some of the older kids went to him and tried to wake him up, but he was out cold. He didn't seem to have any broken bones, and he wasn't bleeding anywhere, so they figured that he was just knocked out. Instead of taking him home, where our house was just around the corner less than a half a block away, Daniel and his older brother, David, carried him to the Chinese bunkhouse and sat him in his desk. That's where Bert woke up before the teacher came into the room. His whole body was sore, and he had a huge headache, but he survived the incident without the teacher or our parents learning about it.

There was another hill we called "Dead Man's Hill" that few brave ones would take a chance on sliding from the very top.

It was across from the new school, and most of us would only go halfway up and slide back down; even at halfway it was wicked if one had a fast sled, because of the huge bumps on the trail. The real challenge started at the very top in front of Johnny Bremner's house. Bert and his friends, Ted Valle and Billy Williams, were two of only a few that would slide the hill. The hill was a forty-five degree angle and about a hundred yards long. They would get a few paces above the starting point at the top of the hill and run as fast as they could, holding their sled to their side; then when the hill started its dip they would flop their sled onto the snow and jump on it. The more speed you got at the top running, the more speed you would gather as you proceeded down the hill. Sometimes people would chicken out and deliberately run into the snow banks, or fall off the sled. I'd seen my brother do all three, but I also witnessed him make it all the way down in complete control and triumph.

If we weren't sledding in the winter months, then we were probably ice skating at the lake behind John Bremner's house. It was a big lake with a large rock island right in the middle, where the adults would build a big bonfire, and roast marshmallows, or hot dogs. On weekends, when the weather was clear, it wasn't unusual to have about twenty or thirty people on the lake. Whole families would be out, either on sleds pulled by dogs, or parents would pull their kids on sleds.

Now it isn't unusual for Yakutat to have eight to ten feet of snow during a typical winter, which would keep people stranded indoors for weeks sometimes. This was why whole families would get out and enjoy the weather when it was good.

In February, what we call candlefish would spawn their eggs on the sandy beach at the head of Monti Bay. It was a fun time for us, and also broke the monotony of the slow, dark and dreary winter months. We would catch these little fish at night with dip nets of every make and size. I saw a lot of the more elaborate nets that were made by the old timers to coffee cans with a bunch of holes punched in it and a handle tied onto it. Us kids would spend hours at a time flashing our flashlights and lanterns into the water, staying as still as we could, and wait for the fish to swim in huge schools along the shore. Then we'd start dipping our nets after them. The running and splashing in the water got us all wet, but it was that time of the year when it warmed up after a few weeks of cold spells during January. It got cold enough, however, for our pant legs to freeze a radiant white. Our hands would also be numb from the cold, but we endured it because we were having so much fun; we had more fun doing this than anything I could remember for this time of the year. Then we would take the fish to the homes in the community, and whatever we had left we'd take home and Mom would roll them in flour and fry these little fish in butter to a golden brown. They were so tasty with steamed rice and cream-style corn. Because the runs lasted for only a week or so and then they'd be gone, we ate these fish until they were coming out of our ears; but it was a once-in-a-year thing so we looked forward to the next season.

It was the same with hooligans. They came around March, but they ran into the rivers and the men would bring them in from the Situk River. If there was a lot of snow, they would walk the ten miles to the Situk pulling sleds, and return with gunnysacks full of hooligan. The fish would be shared with the community and we would eat fried hooligans with rice and corn. They tasted much like candlefish, but were larger. Grandma Minnie and my mother would smoke and dry them and they would be available throughout the rest of the year to take out of the freezer and enjoy on occasion.

In April and May the herring would arrive. Again us kids, particularly Joe and I, would have a ball snagging them with treble hooks. Later they would spawn their eggs on hemlock branches that had been set out by the men, or on certain kinds of kelp. Herring eggs were a real treat and delicacy among our people. Today in Southeast Alaska it is a highly commercialized industry and marketed to Japan.

As I got older, I even got caught up in this subsistence kind of lifestyle, of becoming a gopher or gatherer of Native foods.

I guess there's a kind of unspoken code in every small community. If you are physically fit, and you know there are many elderly people that cannot get out, then you became their arms and legs, whether you realized it or not. Anyway, I always felt that if I was able to catch a salmon in the stream, then I should share it with others, and that is what I have always done.

When the signs of spring showed, the biggest events for us kids were the marble games and tournaments. Even before the snow was gone, we would clear areas along the main road and play marbles. There would be several groups of people all along the road, engaged in this early spring festivity. The games would last from morning fill dark. Sometimes there would be as many as twenty people, both adults and children alike, gathered around this circle in the dirt road below our house. There were a few of the old-timers, like Joe Nelson's stepdad, Sampson Harry, who were great shooters and would challenge us younger boys to a friendly game of marbles. These contests would translate into tournaments that would sometimes last up to six hours or more in a day. My friend, Joe Nelson, and I were probably two of the best shooters, especially when it came to using "steelies" (ball bearings). I can still remember phrases like, "three knuckles high," and "no fudging." Even my dad used to join in sometimes, especially on the weekends when he wasn't working. One of his favorite sayings was, "Three knuckles high, one hand in your back pocket, and both feet off the ground." Joe tried doing this one time and it was a sight to see how his body was twisted in all kinds of contortions. Those were truly some of the most enlightening times when both parents and their children would be playing marbles together.

I must have had a collection of over 1,000 marbles of all sizes and colors. We used to trade each other for some of the larger "steelies," which were the pride and joy of every child, along with the larger-size glass marbles.

Bert wasn't much of a marble player. He admitted this openly, and even though he had his collection of marbles, it wasn't as extensive or impressive as Joe's and mine. One thing that Bert was probably better at than anyone else, other than his friend Ted Valle, was making model airplanes. Whenever he earned enough money, he would go to Helen Bremner's toy store and buy a kit and would spend hours constructing those model airplanes. He took a lot of pride in his work, but when he finished them and flew them for a while, he would go to the upstairs of our house and fly the model out of the window with a firecracker lit in the cowling. The plane would fly for a spell and when the firecracker exploded, the plane would fall apart and spiral down to the ground. Then he'd start on another model.

Other than the marble games, we used to get ourselves into all kinds of mischief, and trouble. On weekends, in the wintertime, we would sneak into the cannery and open cases of canning lids and toss them around like Frisbees. Of course, they were all rusty and would be thrown out anyway, but we. sure made a mess of the whole cannery. It's a wonder no one got seriously hurt, because we used to climb around the rafters, exploring every inch of the cannery.

In the spring we would gather seaweed and gumboots, and in the summer months we'd fish for salmon and halibut. The seaweed would be dried in the sun and put into plastic bags to be distributed to families in the community. The salmon would be either smoked or canned and the halibut would be dried or frozen.

As far as I can remember, we also lived off the land and sea, a subsistence lifestyle which was supplemented by the more traditional food, mainly rice and potatoes, flour, sugar, coffee, tea and the like. It seemed like there were certain groups of people that would go out almost every week gathering clams, cockles, sea urchins, and to hunt seal or deer and distribute their catch to every family in the community. Even though we were caught up in the commercialization of our resources, we also enjoyed participating in the subsistence lifestyle; we shared with one another and this made it appear that the community was like one big family, helping each other through the lean times of the long winter months.

Like the diamonds in the sky, they seem to dance to a different tune.

Stars

Stars are like giant diamonds in the sky at night.
They dazzle us with their sparkling array of colors.
We make a wish whenever we see one falling,
And hope that special wish will soon come true.
But we soon forget what we wished that night,
I for one don't keep track of my many wishes.
I'd like to think all my wishes have been granted,
Even though I haven't gotten my million dollars yet,
On a wish I made way back when I was just a kid.
Then again, come to think of it, maybe I have,
A wish—a hope—a dream—an imagination
is worth more than all the money I could ever want.

11

Life on the Alsek River

"Ha ha," Bert teased. "I'm going to Dry Bay with Dad, and you're not."

"I'm going too." I stomped my foot.

In a sense we were both right because Dad and Bert were going to go first. As Bert got himself ready to go downstairs to meet Dad, he picked up his packsack and said, "But you're not coming out until July."

Under my breath I said, "I want to go now."

I was only seven years old and as I looked at the logic of it now, it only made sense that Bert would go with Dad first. Bert was ten, a little older and mature and would be more helpful to Dad. On the other hand, being the adventurous spirit that I am, I would more likely have been distracted by most anything new in this place we learned to call God's country.

That was in the spring of 1947. The Dry Bay king salmon had begun to run around the middle of April, and the commercial fishing would begin in Dry Bay on May first. Going to Dry Bay was the most important adventure that I was looking forward to and it was hardly bearable for me to watch Dad and Bert take their final belongings down to the dock, Bert proudly walking beside our Dad. He was going out into the wild country to learn how to be a man like our father, and I couldn't keep myself from choking back tears as I saw them walk down the road and onto the bridge from the road that connected the store. They disappeared down a stairway onto the dock. In a short while they re-appeared on the front of the dock and walked to the ladder that would take them to the cannery tender, *Alsek*. The *Alsek* was a beautiful white sixty-foot vessel owned by Fred Erickson. He was an independent fish buyer who lived in Seattle during the winter, and Dad decided he would sell his fish to him this summer because he had gotten into some dispute or disagreement with the cannery people.

I watched with envy as Dad tied a line onto Bert's packsack and lowered it to the deck of the *Alsek*. The *Alsek*'s engine was warming and I could see the white smoke fluffing out of the exhaust stack and hear the low humming of the engine. People were working on the deck. The deck was loaded with four gas boats and the men were tying them snug to the deck. Dad and Bert climbed down the ladder, and in a few minutes the lines were untied and the *Alsek* moved ahead alongside the dock, began to make a turn and then circled until it was heading down the middle of Monti Bay, her bow pointed to the mouth. I could see Dad standing on the bow and Bert was inside the cabin looking out the galley door. He was waving to us. I waved back, and I heard Mom say, "Goodbye, son."

Needless to say, I tried my darndest to keep myself occupied enough to not think too much about the fun Bert was having with my Dad. July couldn't come fast enough.

But it finally came—slow as it did—it arrived and Mom and I boarded the *Alsek*. It was a beautiful afternoon. Watching the men on the deck coiling lines, each person doing their thing, kept me so busy that I didn't realize that we were leaving the entrance of Monti Bay. My first indication was when we were between Ankow and Khantaak Island and we rose under a small wave and then the nose of the *Alsek* dipped down, rose again and dipped. As we got further into Yakutat Bay and began to turn around Point Carew toward Ocean Cape, not only were the waves getting higher, but also the *Alsek* began to roll from one side to the other. We were in the galley; Mom was sitting at the table talking to the cook. My stomach began to churn.

"What's wrong, Pops?" Mom looked at me and could tell I wasn't feeling too good. I didn't answer. "Are you feeling alright?" she asked.

When I tried to answer her, instead of words coming out my whole stomach ended up on the floor of the galley.

"Oh my gosh," Mom said, throwing a towel over the pancakes she fed me earlier that morning.

Well, I have to say that I was never able to overcome seasickness. My brother, Bert, got seasick on his first trip to Dry Bay, but after that he was cured. As for me every time I got on the boat for the long trip to Dry Bay the first place I would head for was an empty bunk and I stayed there until I was sure that we were at anchor in Dry Bay or tied next to the dock in Yakutat. After that I was fine.

When we arrived at Dry Bay, and I had gotten out of bed, I was amazed at how bare the Dry Bay Delta was. On this clear day I could see both mountains, Mount Fairweather to the south, two hundred miles toward Yakutat was Mount Saint Elias, and several miles inland between the mountains was what is known as the St. Elias Range, a line of snow-capped mountains that served was what the borderline between Alaska and Canada.

"Where's the Alsek River?" I asked. That was where Dad and Bert were, and I couldn't see it—everything was so flat here.

"It's up there," Mom said, pointing toward the mountains. "See that gas boat coming down?"

I could see it all right, and then the sound of the engine ringing in my ears.

"It must be Bert and Dad," I said.

I ran along the cabin to the front of the *Alsek* and watched and waited. It was such a beautiful day and I had never seen so many seals at one time. They were all along the bay, some swimming along and others in small groups. And then in the air, there were millions of seagulls. Along the sand spit that separated the bay from the ocean were fish camp—tents that were huddled together and each one surrounded with a series of logs constructed on the southerly side so the strong southeasterly winds would not blow them away. Along the shoreline were about seven gas boats anchored, swaying this way and that way as the currents of the wind or the shift of the water from the tide that created eddies along the shore. This was a beautiful sight.

The gas boat came closer and sure enough I recognized Bert at the bow and Dad's dark yarn hat which blended in with his thick, black beard. It seemed that all I could see above his face was the whites of his eyes.

"Hi, Pops! Hi, Mom!" Bert hollered.

Mom and Dad hugged and kissed. Bert and I were glad to see each other and we slapped each other on the back. After loading all our belongings we brought from town, we jumped into the gas boat and Dad headed us upriver to our camp.

"The camp is right at the mouth of Williams Creek," Bert said to me. We both shared a spot at the bow of the gas boat. Seals were swimming and bobbing all around us, and Bert said that all we needed to do was point our finger to them and they'd dive into the water.

"When you point a finger at them," Bert said, "they think you're pointing a gun and so that's why they dive."

When we traveled a long way up, we could see where the channel of the Alsek emptied into Dry Bay. Lots of stumps were stuck in the gravel riverbed, and the swift current of the Alsek caused large wakes that made them appear as if they were barging their way upriver. We could see small icebergs drifting by. They had broken off from larger ones further up, and Dad would sometimes have to dodge those that were clumped close together.

We were going to be staying with an old-timer by the name of Bill Geddes, who had been fishing in this area for many years. He had a large cabin and became very close friends with Dad, so he invited all of us to stay with him for the next summer and winter.

Bill's cabin was located about five miles upriver, on a high rocky knoll overlooking the entire river. I remember the cabin as being large, almost like a barn. There was a shed attached to the entryway where the front door opened into a large kitchen and dining room. Off to the right was this huge room, divided into four sections by drapes which hung from the ceiling; off to the left, as you entered the bedroom area was a pot-bellied wood stove, and near the center of the room was this trap door in the floor; a ladder led down to a dark cellar, where all the food was stored.

Outside, off to the side of the cabin was a large garden, where Bill grew his own vegetables. He grew the largest cabbages, potatoes, carrots, turnips, rutabagas, and radishes I ever saw.

The cabin was built in and among the alders, just below the heavy timber on this huge rocky knoll. There was a clearing on this knoll about a hundred yards from the cabin where you could stand and look out over the entire river, about five miles downstream.

Just to the left of the clearing was the biggest cottonwood tree I believe I have ever seen, and I immediately claimed it as my very own lookout post. Here I spent many days building a tree house, complete with a rope ladder and an emergency escape route (a large rope with knots tied in it about every two feet).

We lived off the land for the whole year we stayed there, supplementing our diet with such staples as rice, flour, sugar, canned milk, etc., which we had flown in from Yakutat by a bush pilot during his weekly mail run in the winter months.

Bill and Dad trapped and hunted for fur-bearing game.

They made their own snowshoes; Bill had an old-fashioned sled they used for hauling their traps and food stuff.

Dad even made a pair of skis for him and Bill out of 2x4's. Now this might seem impossible, but I learned one thing about our dad—nothing is impossible if you have ingenuity. He was able to somehow split the 2x4's in half. Then he planed them to the right width and sanded them smooth. Then the ingenuity came by him sticking about a foot and a half of the ends into boiling water. When he thought they were steamed enough, he was able to bend the ends into a curve. Again, he sanded and polished the bottoms and waxed the skis so that they slid through the snow very easily. He made straps for them to connect their boots onto, and when he was done they were a sight and an accomplishment to behold. One would find it hard to believe that these were made from 2x4's and made to improve tending to their trap lines much faster than using snowshoes and pulling a sled. When conditions were right they were able to slide across the snow and return from their trap lines in a matter of a couple of days where in previous ventures it would take weeks.

That winter, we subsisted on moose, ducks, geese, and rabbit until they were practically coming out of our ears.

Speaking of rabbits, I didn't know for the longest time that people ate rabbits! I remember that whenever we had an excellent dinner, something that was really tasty, I would always compliment Mom and ask what it was. She would always say it was chicken. Needless to say, during that winter, we really ate a lot of chicken.

Every morning Bert and I would wake up to the smell of fresh coffee perking on the wood stove. I always knew that whenever the coffee was done, Mom would soon start making a big batch of sourdough pancakes.

I tell you, we truly became a family during this period in our lives, living in God's country and just living the good life as He intended us to do.

One thing about the Dry Bay area is that when fall was well underway and winter was knocking on the door there would be strong winds that would sweep down from the mountains. I remember one time, I believe it was toward the end of October and into all of November, we started feeling the real impact of those northerly winds. They were strong, cold and gusty—sometimes the gusts would be as strong as fifty to sixty knots. Finally, a week or so before Christmas, the wind let up and the storm passed. However, it started to snow quite hard, which left visibility to almost nothing. Our bush pilot friend radioed us, saying he would bring our mail and Christmas gifts, and drop them by parachute. It was just two days before Christmas when the parachute landed, full of Christmas cards and gifts from our friends in Yakutat.

I can still remember so clearly this one night just a few days before Christmas. Dad had a big bonfire going at the bottom of a big hill not too far from the cabin where we used to ski.

Mom and Dad had made a batch of home brew and decided to roast some ducks, and "chicken" over the bonfire, while my brother and L along with Bill Geddis, were learning how to ski down this hill. We were all having a ball, just whooping it up and falling more times than not, but getting right back up and trying again.

This one time Bill Geddis and I were coming down the hill, side by side, when suddenly, out of nowhere, come this flash of lightning that seemed to light up the whole sky, followed a few seconds later by a loud rumble of thunder.

In mid-stride, halfway down the hill, I let out a scream as loud as the thunder itself, and jumped off my skis and made a beeline directly for the cabin. It had been the very first time I had seen lightning, or heard thunder—but wait, here's the rest of the story.

Old Bill Geddis must have been just as scared as I was because we met at the front door at the same time. I found out later that he had always been afraid of lightning and thunder, saying it's "God's wrath on mankind."

Again, December was the beginning of one of the worst storms that winter. The north wind whipped up something awful, and it didn't let up for three long weeks. During that first week, our bush pilot friend couldn't even fly. The second week the wind let up a little, with gusts up to eighty and a hundred knots. During this storm, Dad and Bill couldn't tend their trap line, so Dad started making our Christmas toys. He made me a beautiful dump truck, complete with a crank to turn that would lift the bed to dump my load of sand or gravel. He made my brother a beautiful model ship of some kind, with all the little details included. Each one of us cherished those toys and kept them for quite a few years.

Now, I must tell you my experience with that parachute. I was only seven years old at the time, and just as scrawny as they come.

One clear sunny day the wind was really gusting pretty well, so I thought I'd try jumping off the rocky cliff to see how softly I'd land on the sand below. I proceeded to get a good running start and let out a loud "whoopee" as I jumped off the cliff just as a gust of wind caught the parachute, and I went straight up, about fifty feet off the ground, screeching like a banshee, too afraid to think of letting go.

Mom, Dad, and Bert could do nothing but watch me! I sailed about 100 yards across the garden area. Mom was screaming, and Dad was hollering to me to "Let go!" He was frantic, running after me.

"Let go, Popeye! Let go!"

Bert was running behind Dad, and I think he was actually crying. Before I got too high into the air I was finally deposited in some alders on the other side of the garden, a little bruised, but otherwise unhurt.

My favorite pastime was playing in my treehouse behind our cabin. Sometimes, when the weather was clear and the northern lights were out, my brother would join me in my treehouse, watching the northern lights and listening to the coyotes off in the distance howling at the moon. Believe me, it made me feel like a primitive man, listening to the coyotes, and watching the wonders of the universe as if they were made for our eyes only.

A typical day for Bill and Dad would begin at daybreak. They would eat a good hearty breakfast and be off to tend their trap line by six A.M. They would return just before dusk each day with their packsack full of furs to be skinned and stretched.

They trapped mostly mink otter, fox, and an occasional wolf or coyote. As I explained earlier, Dad snared plenty of "chicken" for the stew pot.

There was a period, in January when they were unable to tend their trap line for almost a week and a half, because of severe snowstorms. When they were finally able to get out to check the trap line, they found fresh wolverine tracks at almost all of the traps, apparently looking for a fresh-caught meal. However, one of the traps must have been hidden pretty good because the wolverine left his paw and part of his front leg in the trap—he had literally chewed his own leg off to get out of the wolf trap! Dad never ever saw that three-legged wolverine again.

I had my own trap line too, but I didn't even have to go outside of the cabin to catch all the furs I wanted. I was in the weasel-trapping business, using regular mouse traps set up in the corner I could find around the entrance of the shed, and all around the outside of the cabin. I must have caught at least two dozen of those little rascals that winter.

The only real entertainment we had, other than playing solitaire or monopoly, or other games like Scrabble was listening to the different programs on our Sears & Roebuck Zenith short-wave radio. Some of my favorite programs at the time were *The Bickersons, Fibber McGee & Molly, Amos 'n Andy, Art Link-letter, Arthur Godfrey* and *Jack Benny*. Also *Dragnet* and *The Twilight Zone* were two of the evening programs we used to listen to every night. We used to listen to the news of the armed forces radio network.

Anyway, the station call letters were AFRTS, but the announcer said FARTS, and as soon as the announcer said the S, he completely went off the air for about a minute. From that day on, every time Dad would hear the announcer give their call numbers, he would jump up and tell us he was taking a FART break!

Even though we were in Dry Bay that winter because of the school burning down, that didn't free us from learning the three Rs. Mom was a good teacher and she devoted four hours each day teaching us arithmetic, reading and writing. We especially enjoyed Mom reading to us *The Adventures of Tom Sawyer* and *Huckleberry Finn*.

All during this time in Dry Bay, Mom and Dad used to make home brew on a regular basis; however, I don't remember seeing either of them get drunk like they used to in Yakutat.

They sure would get a lot of seagulls drunk though every time they would dump their barrel of raisins or whatever. I can still see this swarm of seagulls converge on this mound of raisins like vultures, gorging themselves until they couldn't even fly. Some would be flapping their wings and just fall on their faces. Others would sort of waddle off and just fall over, their feet kicking, and their heads just rolling from side to side, as if they were laughing at a good joke or something. It really was a sight to behold!

That summer Dad moved us a couple miles downriver where he built a cabin that was near the edge of a bank over a slough. Dad had nets set out in the slough where he fished for king salmon in early spring and sockeyes in the summer. Every day Bert and I would have to stand watch for the pick-up scow to arrive on his daily rounds, picking up the day's catch from every family on the river to be delivered to the fish tender, the *Italio*, anchored at the mouth of the river.

Whenever we'd see the familiar square cabin on the thirty-two-foot flat-bottomed river scow, we'd have to go tell Dad, because it took him about ten to fifteen minutes to walk from the cabin to the skiffs where the fish were kept.

It seemed like we'd always tag along with Dad when he'd go to pitch his day's catch onto the pick-up scow—rain or shine because Gunnar Erickson would have candy bars or some goodies for us.

The cannery tender, *Italio*, was captained by an old-timer we nicknamed Captain Stuck, because he was always halfway drunk, and would always get stuck on a sand bar while coming into the mouth of the river, where the river empties out into the Pacific Ocean. Every Friday the *Italio* would haul the week's catch into Yakutat to be delivered to the cannery for processing. The *Italio* would return on Sunday afternoon or evening, bringing whatever groceries or supplies the fishermen may have ordered for that week. The whole family would go with Dad downriver on Sundays to pick up our supplies of groceries and fuel for the coming week.

Almost always, Dad would order whiskey, and whenever it came time to head back upriver to our cabin, it would always be late and dark.

Dad would be pretty well looped by then and although he knew the river well, he would almost always hit at least one sand bar. Either Bert or I would sit right at the bow of our gas boat, pointing the way to Dad.

There was one time though, it was real foggy, and old Bill

71

Geddis and Dad were just singing to their hearts' content, with me at the bow trying to shout directions, and he couldn't hear a word I was saying. We hit a sand bar and couldn't back off of it so I jumped off the bow of the skiff into the blackness, thinking I'd push us off the sand bar without any problem!

Well, I didn't jump out directly in front of the skiff, but off to the side where the river just dropped off into deep water!

I never did hit bottom, but sure popped straight up out of the icy water like a cork, trying to catch my breath as I crawled into the skiff. We eventually made it home, but I think I almost froze; I was so cold and wet.

Before the fishing season was over, Dad had told us boys that we would be moving back to Yakutat in September because Bert and I needed to get back to school and that he would, once again, be working for the FAA operating heavy equipment.

So, in the fall of 1948, we moved back to civilization where my brother and I continued our schooling.

Self-explanatory, simple is easier. Always remember to be as simple as possible in all you do in life

I'm a Simple Man

Simple words, when put together right,
Make a very simple statement.
I'm simple, not into fancy, meaningless words,
Because, simply put —they stink!
Fancy words just cloud the simple issue,
And that's simply not my style.
My simple lifestyle has taught me to
Appreciate the simpler things of life.
That's why all my writings are so simple.
And simply speaking—in my own opinion,
Simple words just make a lot more sense.
It's simply amazing, don't you think,
How simple these simple words are.

12

Life on the Situk and Ahrnklin Rivers

Dad got his job back with the FAA, but it wasn't too long before he was threatened with termination because of his drinking problems.

I honestly believe that both Mom and Dad had made a great sacrifice for us boys to continue our education in Yakutat. I know that they had always loved fishing and in those days fishing was fast becoming the economic boom for the whole Yakutat area.

I remember hearing them argue a lot during that fall and winter of 1948–1949, and about whether they should just move back out to Dry Bay and leave us boys to stay with Dad's mother until school was out.

They finally decided they would "stick it out" until early spring, when Dad would quit his job and we all would try fishing in the Situk River about ten miles out of town.

The Situk and Ahrnklin Rivers were actually two separate rivers that converged as one, emptying into the Pacific Ocean about ten miles southeast of Yakutat along the coastline. This was where about 90 percent of the population fished during the summer months.

This was why Libby-McNeill & Libby had built a railroad to the head of the Situk River in the early 1900s. This railroad ran directly from the dock downtown, ten miles through the brush and timber, finally ending at the headwaters of the Situk River.

The train, as we called it, was a real-live steam locomotive that was probably already an antique when purchased, but it pulled about two freight cars and about three or four flat cars. The freight cars were just flat cars with four walls on them.

These were used to haul "skiffs" and "outboard motors" along with groceries and about one to two hundred "passengers" to the Situk River every Sunday afternoon. The majority of the fishermen came back into their homes at the close of the weekly fishing period, which was on Fridays, so the community would be like a ghost town from Sundays through Fridays of each week, and like a wild party town from Friday evenings through Sunday when the whole ritual would start over again.

I must tell you, living and fishing out on the Situk River in those days was like living in a tent city. It seemed like there must have been well over fifty tents, plus a few permanent cabins, all up and along the edge of the river and along the sandy beaches on the Ahrnklin River side.

A lot of us kids used to play in the woods building tree-houses, swings, and forts for our war games.

This was also when we got caught in the act of learning to smoke cigarettes. I must relate this incident to you, as I clearly remember it.

I was nine years old at the time and my brother was twelve. We lived in our own tent which Dad had set up not more than ten feet away from their tent. It was on a Sunday afternoon and we thought Mom and Dad were too sick from a hangover to get out of bed so my brother and I started smoking cigarette butts gathered from around the tent, and began to play blackjack.

We must have looked a sight as we each had caps on with cigarette butts dangling from our mouths as we sat around this cardboard box saying, "Hit me!" or "Hit me again!"

My brother was facing the tent opening and I had my back to the entrance. We were having a great time puffing away with the whole interior of the tent filled with thick cigarette smoke.

Suddenly, just as I said, "Hit me!" my brother's eyes bulged out, and his mouth dropped open with his cigarette dangling on his lower lip. He just stared at the tent opening behind me in complete silence. As I turned around to see what Bert was staring at, there was Dad, peeking into the tent flap opening.

We were caught and we were caught good as Dad glared at each of us and said, "I'll be right back." And then he left.

He returned in a few minutes with a full pack of Mom's cigarettes and pulled up a stool as he sat down and opened the pack of cigarettes. "Okay, boys," he said. "Deal me in." Now Dad didn't smoke at all and couldn't stand cigarette smoke, especially when he was hungover. "Okay, boys," he said, "you want to be like grownups, huh? Have to smoke like grownups, huh? Come on boys, deal me in." And then he offered us each a cigarette.

For the rest of the afternoon we sat there while he made us all smoke one cigarette after another while we played game after game of poker. It seemed it took us forever to finish off that pack because we were so sick and coughing so much, but we finally did finish the day in that smoky tent. When we were done Dad left without saying a single word, but we could hear him behind the tent tossing his cookies. I think he was sicker than we were, but he didn't want to show it while we were playing poker.

Dad never said another word about that incident, but Mom told us some time later just how sick he really got. My brother and I didn't touch a cigarette until we were in our late teens and whenever a cigarette was offered to me I always remembered that special incident when Dad taught my brother and me an important lesson through his example.

I am told the moon is artificial, but the real mystery is, is it reflection of light or?

The Moon

Man has walked on its surface with glee,
Like a child in a sandbox full of strange soil,
They say the moon has mystical, magical powers,
The fact it is even there is a real mystery to me,
It is called the planet of love and romance,
A full moon does awaken man's inner being,
They say it gets its light solely from the sun,
But at nighttime, just where is the sun,
I think therein lies the real mystery,
Einstein I am not, but anyone can see,
The source of its power comes from you and me.

13

We Move to Akwe River

Well, all good things must come to an end sooner or later. In the spring of 1950, we moved to the Akwe River, another fishing river about twelve miles from Dry Bay toward Yakutat.

Dad felt he had to have some help so he hired two of his friends as partners for the summer. Their names were Peter Harry, and Alex Johnson. They were like a part of our family, helping Dad with all the strenuous tasks of setting tents for a total of six people, building windbreakers around the tents, and hauling all the necessary equipment to accommodate our needs.

There was no fish tender in the Akwe River because it is too small for any kind of tender to enter so we were told our fish would have to be flown out by airplane on a regular schedule of twice a day, at least until the cannery was able to work out a plan of having a fish tender stationed in the Alsek, or Dry Bay River. This meant that we had to have a truck of some kind to haul our fish to the ocean beach, where the airplane would have to land, or haul our fish to Dry Bay.

Our first truck was a surplus military Willis Jeep, with a small truck bed—the kind that had the four boxes in back for carrying extra cans of fuel. The Jeep came equipped with a front-mounted winch and extra-wide tires, which gave good traction in the soft sand.

We had four skiffs and outboards, a canoe which was rented to me by Dad's friends, and our Jeep along with all the necessary tents, lumber, equipment, and fishing gear needed to supply us for the whole summer. We also had about six drums of gas for the truck and outboards. It was early April when all of our equipment was loaded onto a military type LC5 or landing craft, the type where the front drops down to off-load vehicles.

As we left the Yakutat harbor, I couldn't help but think we were going on some kind of military mission instead of beginning a whole new way of life living in God's country.

That summer happened to be my first experience of fishing on my own. I was eleven years old at the time and Dad's friends equipped me with a ten-fathom net and a canoe which they rented to me for $100 for the entire fishing season. I didn't have an outboard so I had to use oars for getting around. Dad's friends used to tease me a lot saying they could lease me an outboard motor and it would cost me another $500 . . . I preferred to use my own two-horse power "armstrong."

I remember settlement time, standing behind Dad and his friend as they received their earnings for the summer. I was told earlier that I made about $100 but was not prepared for the prank Dad's friends pulled on me. They handed me this piece of paper that had an itemized list of expenses they incurred for outfitting me for the entire summer. Their list included $100 for the canoe rental, $50 for oars and oar locks, $50 for an anchor and lines, $50 for two-dozen pair of gloves and of course they had to include moorage and maintenance fees. When it was all added up I owed them $200 after my $100 income. After they had their laugh and because I was almost in tears, they tore up the expense list and handed me two one-hundred-dollar bills, which really changed my disposition real fast.

During that summer, our fish was picked up and delivered by plane to the airport in Yakutat, then hauled to town by truck, where it was finally delivered to the local cannery. We were told to expect a pick-up twice a day, at eight A.M. and again at eight P.M.

The only thing we didn't know was what kind of airplane they would send and where would it land, until it actually arrived. Sometimes it would be a PBY that would land in the river or it might be a DC-3 which would have to land on the ocean beach. We actually had a pool going trying to guess which plane would show up and where it would land.

Of course the cannery soon realized that this method of delivery was too costly and decided to put a fish tender in Dry Bay because the Akwe River was too small for any kind of fish tender to enter the river.

It was sometime in August of 1950 when we began to haul our fish to Dry Bay, a seventeen-mile drive each way through the sand and tundra driving through some of the most beautiful scenery in God's country.

This stretch of sand and grass, with strawberries everywhere, surrounded by patches of alders disbursed among the spruce and hemlock trees, was only about a quarter of a mile wide from the ocean to the heavy timber of the Tongass National Forest.

This area is truly God's country with the ever-present majestic Mt. Fairweather looming almost straight ahead toward Dry Bay.

The best way I can describe the Mt. St. Elias and Mt. Fairweather mountain ranges total area is like this: If a person stood facing the center of the mountain range with both hands outstretched to the sides, your right hand would be pointing directly at Mt. Fairweather, and your left hand would be pointing at Mt. St. Elias. The distance between the two mountains is probably 150 miles or so.

There is an area about halfway to Dry Bay that we call the "badlands," because the road goes through some heavy timber and small lakes as the road twists and turns in a series of curves around dead falls in the timber and alders. This area is where we could almost count on seeing plenty of bear, simply because it was closest to their natural feeding grounds. We used to throw out a lot of scrap in this area and it seemed like the bears knew when we were coming by because every time we'd pass by there would be a group here and there looking for handouts.

There were many times while picking strawberries that a dog literally saved me from walking right up on a bear in the brush, who was also picking strawberries.

Speaking of strawberries, Mom used to make plenty of strawberry cream puffs. They would literally melt in your mouth and just thinking about them right now is making my mouth water.

When we first moved to the Akwe we were all so amazed and overwhelmed at the beauty of the area, with the ever-present roar of the ocean surf pounding on the sandy beach.

Sometime in mid-July the weather was unusually warm for about two weeks; the temperature was in the high 70s and 80s. My brother and I thought nothing of playing in the ocean waves, being tumbled around like a barrel, and washed up onto the beach. Although the water was ice cold, we enjoyed the tumbling action of the waves, not knowing a thing about the strong undertow.

This one particular day the waves were quite large, apparently due to high winds out in the gulf. My brother and I would wade out to our waist and as a large wave crested we would dive tight into the wave and be tumbled around, finally being deposited on the beach. I was waiting for a good wave as I waded out, watching a large wave cresting right in front of me.

This was the granddaddy of all waves and as I dove into the wave I felt like I hit a solid wall as I was carried to the very top of the wave and rode the crest, until it came crashing down on the sandy beach, completely knocking all the wind out of me. As the wave receded I was so stunned and helpless it rolled me out into the deeper water where the undertow caught me. No matter how hard I tried I felt like a lead weight being tossed-around under water, losing air supply.

My brother saw that I was in trouble and was thrashing around, trying to find me. just as I was about to lose consciousness, I felt something grab my leg and I was pulled to the surface, both of us gasping for air, as we were tossed onto the shore too exhausted to move. I don't need to tell you that we learned to respect the ocean and never played in the surf after that.

I wasn't aware of the fact that Dad had two daughters from a previous marriage who were living in Wrangell until sometime in 1951. We had been fishing in the Akwe River when Dad apparently received a letter from them saying they wanted to meet their real dad. Of course their mother was remarried and the girls had been adopted by their new dad, Bill Stokes, but they were both at the age where they were curious about who their real dad was.

They were allowed to come up from Wrangell, Alaska the summer of 1951 for a two-week visit.

The two weeks before their visit, we helped Dad set up a new tent for our newly found family and even planned out a daily schedule of events, or outings, during the girls' two week stay. We were all ecstatic, realizing that we would soon be meeting two girls named Juanita and Myrna, whom Dad had not seen since they were about one or two years old. Dad had explained that Juanita was now fifteen and Myrna was fourteen and since my brother was fourteen and I was eleven, we should all get along fine.

The big day finally came and as we all jumped into our truck to head for the ocean beach, where the plane would land, Dad was a nervous wreck, trying his best to keep composed by telling jokes or stories, but at the same time the tears would just come pouring out of his eyes.

As the small plane landed and taxied up by our truck, we

were all anxiously awaiting the arrival of these two young girls, but were quite shocked to see two young ladies get out of the small plane.

It was quite a scene to behold, all of us huddled around each other, watching Juanita and Myrna hugging Dad and all three of them just bawling like babies. Pretty soon we were all crying our hearts out, caught up in the emotional event.

Finally, after all the introductions were made, we invited the pilot, a Mr. Butch Vent, to have dinner with us. Mom had prepared a nice big moose roast with mashed potatoes and gravy, all topped off with freshly baked banana cream pie.

I was quite amazed and impressed with how much both Juanita and Myrna resembled Dad, in both looks and character. Both of them had a sense of humor that just wouldn't quit, telling jokes and stories about certain incidents in their lives, making us all laugh so hard.

The next two weeks were as if we were on some kind of vacation, where all normal routine chores were set aside, making every moment revolve around Juanita and Myrna's every whim or wish. One day might be spent driving along the ocean beach, zigzagging the waves as they'd wash up on the beach, just beach combing for glass balls or whatever. Another day would be set aside for a picnic way upriver while fishing for cutthroat and rainbow trout. No matter what we had planned each day, there was always a bear sighting and the girls would have to take a bunch of pictures. They must have gone through a dozen rolls of film apiece during their two-week stay.

We picked strawberries and Mom taught the girls how to make strawberry cream puffs, which were a favorite dessert of Dad's and mine, next to banana cream pie.

The time finally arrived when the girls had to return home to Wrangell and amidst more shedding of tears and hugs and feelings of sadness, we watched the small plane take off with Juanita and Myna, not knowing if we'd ever see them again. We knew Dad was having a hard time so when he took off in the truck after taking Mom, my brother and me back to camp, no one said a single word. To this day, no one ever asked, nor were we told why Dad ever left his first wife with his two daughters.

In the nine summers spent on the Akwe River I don't think there is any one area that we didn't explore throughout the whole ten- to fifteen-mile area from the mouth of the Akwe to Dry Bay. If the tide was low, Dad would always want to drive on the ocean beach, in the hard-sand beach, zigzagging in and out of the ocean waves. We could just about double our speed on the hard sand, and it was almost a straight run instead of the constant turns and curves in the main road near the heavy timber. This meant we were able to do about forty or fifty miles an hour compared to the twenty or thirty miles per hour on the main road, and making it to Dry Bay in about forty-five minutes instead of the one and a half or two hours.

However, Dad would always throw caution to the wind and start playing tag with the waves as they rolled in and out. There were several times a wave would catch us just right and flood the engine.

I remember many times when I would have to run the three or four miles to our neighbor's camp in Akwe to have them come and pull us out of the surf before the tide would completely engulf us. We soon learned to carry a can of starting fluid with us and if we got caught in a wave and the engine died on us, we'd just squirt some starting fluid into the carburetor and in no time be off and running again.

As the years went by Dad learned real fast not to play tag with the ocean waves on the beach, and very seldom went down to the beach, except to search for Japanese glass balls that were regularly found on the beaches.

If we only knew then what these glass balls would be worth

to the tourists and collectors we would have been able to retire in that first year. Of course that wasn't the case though because we only collected them because they were there. They served only as a conversation piece, not as decorative pieces in our cabin when we finally left Akwe in 1959.

When Mom and Dad would drink, they'd always want to drive over to Dry Bay and visit friends and get more booze. It seemed like they never cared whether it was day or night, but whenever they'd get the urge to go, my brother and I would always go with them.

We've all grown up with a favorite pet of one kind or another, as carefree as can be.

Buck

My dog, Buck, was part Cocker Spaniel
and part St. Bernard.
He was my friend, my partner, and confidant, too.
I used to talk to him as if he really knew
I think back on it now and I think he understood
What was expected of him at the right time and place.
He used to sit up and beg, and fetch a ball
Or play dead if I went "bang"
with my finger pointed to his head.
He'd sit and stare at a piece of candy on my knee
With drool coming down his cheeks,
he'd look, but not touch
'Til I gave him the signal that it was all right to eat.
He hated bear with a passion and used to chase
Them all over the place and jump on their back
And hang on for dear life 'til the bear stopped running.
Then he'd jump off and make a beeline for me
Which was a bad idea because
the bear was now chasing him.
Oh, we sure had fun growing up together
Just the two of us, as carefree as can be
My dog, Buck—and me.

14

Our Pet Dogs

It seemed we always had a dog as a pet. The first one I actually remember was a large brown female dog we called Queenie. Maybe it was just because I was quite young at the time, but she was a huge dog, taking up the whole front porch.

Queenie was Dad's dog and not allowed in the house because she was so huge. Every morning as Dad got ready for work he would feed her and she would follow him down to the dock where he would catch a ride to work, some five miles away to the airport.

As soon as Dad would leave for work, Queenie would wander up to the Libby McNeil & Libby bunkhouses, which were about a quarter mile out of town on a high hill overlooking the town. She would make her rounds, raiding the garbage cans in the area, and we wouldn't see her again until late afternoon, just before Dad would come home from work.

I clearly remember one stormy winter Saturday afternoon; we heard Queenie whining at the door so pitiful, banging the front door with what sounded like chains. Dad went to see what all the commotion was about, and there was Queenie holding up her front left paw, which was firmly caught in a wolf trap. She apparently managed to break the chain loose and hobbled all the way home. Dad freed her from the trap and soaked her paw in cold water and bandaged her up. She hobbled around for a while, but was fine after a few days of tender loving care.

Another incident I remember involving Queenie was when she saved a man's life by attacking a large brown bear and chasing it away just before it had attacked the man. The older gentleman was the night watchman for the cannery and lived in a cabin in the woods up near the bunkhouse area where Queenie used to make her rounds raiding the garbage cans.

One morning while walking along the path through the woods toward his cabin, a large brown bear had come up right behind him and was just about to give him a bear hug of sorts. Just as the bear was about to rear up on its hind legs, Queenie jumped on the bear from behind and sunk her teeth into the bear's neck with a vice-like grip. This startled the bear long enough for the old man to run to his cabin. Queenie managed to stay away from the bear's lunges as it turned on Queenie, chasing her deep into the woods.

It was only a matter of a few minutes before the old man exited his cabin and fired a couple of rounds from his 30-06 into the air. Apparently, the shots startled the bear long enough for Queenie to make it back to the cabin, exhausted but unhurt. The old night watchman was so thankful that he let Queenie into his house and fed her a big steak he had planned to cook for himself. The next morning Queenie wouldn't leave the area after the old man let her out, thinking Queenie would wander back home to our place.

That evening the old man was waiting for Dad as he came home from work—waiting to tell him how Queenie had saved his life and wouldn't leave the area of his cabin. Dad listened to the old man's story, and didn't have the heart to take Queenie back, so he told the old man he could keep Queenie.

The next dog I remember was a brown mongrel Dad named Mike. He was definitely Dad's dog. I believe Dad got him for protection for us when we moved to Dry Bay that summer. He was very aggressive to anyone that came near Dad if he didn't know who they were, and this proved to be fatal.

When we first got Mike as a pup, there were two young men who worked at the cannery who used to poke sticks at him as they walked by the house each day on their way to work. We took Mike out to Dry Bay one summer and when we returned to town the following fall he was a full-grown dog. He apparently remembered those two guys as they walked by the house on their way to work. He took after them, yelping and barking as if they were his next meal. He chased them all the way down the road and they just barely made it into the cannery store. From that day on those two guys used to take the long route on the back road behind our house to go to work.

I mentioned earlier that Mike was a very possessive dog and Dad was his master. It was early spring when one of our cousins came home from going to school at Mount Edgecumbe High School in Sitka, Alaska. Anyway, Mike didn't know who she was and when Audrey came knocking on the door, Mike started growling and barking at her. As Mom opened the door, Audrey, of course, ran right in and opened her arms to hug Dad. Well, that was too much for Mike to handle as he made a leap and bit Audrey on the thigh, drawing blood.

That was the last time I ever saw Mike, as Dad put him on a chain and with tears in his eyes, grabbed his 30-06 and said he'd be back. He was gone for about an hour and came back by himself. Well, we all knew he had to do what he had to do, so no one said a word about that incident ever again.

It was probably about a year later before we got another dog. It must have been sometime in 1949 or 1950. It was a black-and-white cocker spaniel, mixed with a Saint Bernard; he was about twice the size of Mike.

He was definitely my dog and Dad named him Buck, after the main character in Jack London's novel, *Call of the Wild*. I taught Buck how to sit up, shake hands, roll over, jump through a hoop, retrieve sticks, and of course, sit and stare at a piece of candy I'd place on my knee—with drool coming down his cheeks, his eyes pleading with me, but not touching the piece of candy until I said, "Okay."

Buck hated bears with a passion, and wouldn't hesitate to chase after one while we were driving around the dirt roads in Yakutat. However, Buck was in his glory when I took him to the Akwe River, we would spend the summers fishing. Whenever we would haul our fish over to Dry Bay, Buck would be flopped up on the hood of the truck, swaying back and forth as we made our way along the sandy dirt road. We knew when we would be seeing bears along our path because Buck would stiffen up and the hair on his back would stand straight up. He would sniff the air for their scent and when he spotted a bear he would leap off the hood and chase after the bear. The last we would see of Buck would be him jumping onto a bear's hind end and hanging on for dear life, as they'd disappear into the heavy timber.

Whenever we wanted Buck to come to us, all we'd have to do was whistle real loud and a few minutes later Buck would suddenly appear, making a beeline for the hood of our truck, and hop up onto the hood, ready for more action.

We had Buck all the time we were fishing in the Akwe River from, 1950 until I went to high school at Sheldon Jackson High School in 1955–1956.

Every fall when we would move back into Yakutat, Buck used to follow me to school each morning, waiting on the front porch of the schoolhouse until school was out, to escort me back home.

There was a small convenience store about halfway between our house and the school, where I used to stop and do errands after school before going home. This one morning on my way to school I was making Buck fetch sticks for me as we made our way along the dirt road.

As we passed this store called the Trading Post, owned by Mrs. Simmons, Buck must have been quite peppy. Buck took off running up to the front porch of the store and with his front paws on the doorknob, began to turn the knob until it swung open. Buck went running inside with me right behind him calling out, "Buck! Come here! Come on, Buck! Get out of there!"

The next thing I heard was some high-pitched squealing as Mrs. Simmons came running to the door with a broom, trying to shoo Buck out the door. From that day on, I had to keep Buck on a leash.

In the fall of 1955, after I left for high school at Sheldon Jackson, Buck got sick and had to be put to sleep. That was the last dog I had during those trying times.

Children know just how to make parents give in. It's like magic, isn't it?

Children

Children are truly a miracle from God.
They can make you laugh or cry
With just a certain look on their face.
It may be a twitch of an eyebrow,
Or the droop of a lower lip.
Their expressions are endless
As they become quite a hit,
With family and friends gathered around,
Of parents bonding with their children,
And nurturing them through feeding schedules,
We moan and groan through sleepless nights,
Of burping this child and soothing
The teething pains, of constant diaper changes
And washing out dirty stains.
Somehow, we prevail, though I don't know how.
As parents we are all so gullible, but
Who can ever deny, your child
When they ask you that magic question,
Huh, Mom? Huh, Dad? Can I? Huh, Can I?

15

My Mischievious Teens

In the fall my brother and I were still going to school in Yakutat, but as soon as school was out in May, we would move out to the Akwe River. In 1953, when I was thirteen years old, Dad bought me a brand-new Remington .222 rifle with a 4x Leopold scope. He apparently figured I was now old enough to go out deer hunting or seal hunting with my friend.

In April of that year, my friend Joe Nelson and I went out rabbit hunting along the main road to the airport. He had his .22 Hornet and I had my .222. It was a clear, sunny spring day as we trekked through the woods for most of that afternoon, getting bored because we never saw a single rabbit. We started shooting at these brown glass insulators on the light poles lined up all along the main road that led to the airport, not even thinking or even aware of what they were. We apparently shot enough or ran out of ammunition, I don't know which, but we went home still arguing with each other as to who was the best shot.

The next day my friend and I got called into the principal's office where these two gentlemen in suits were sitting (I knew I must have been in trouble).

These guys started asking us a lot of questions like, "Where were you yesterday, and did you have rifles with you?"

Without hesitation, I began telling these gentlemen where we were and when I starting telling them about shooting the glass insulators on the light poles, their faces cringed with utter disbelief, and their eyes just about bulged out of their sockets.

In our infinite childish wisdom we knocked out all radio communication between the flight service station and all aircraft in the Yakutat area. All flights in and out of Yakutat were canceled for two days while all the communication lines were being repaired. We didn't know it then, but the two guys in suits were FBI agents from Anchorage. We were both severely reprimanded by these two agents and were given quite a lecture about all power poles and insulators. The very next day after all the repairs were made, there were large metal signs posted on every pole in the community.

After fishing ended in 1953 some of us boys would go out to the various salmon creeks in the area and catch red coho salmon as they migrated up to their spawning grounds. We used to give them to the older people around town because they made good boiled fish.

One weekend in October my friends Billy Williams, Lowell Peterson and I went out to a creek about two miles out of town near the airport area. We absconded with one of these obsolete old railroad cars, the kind with a large handle that you push up and down to make the thing move along the track. Billy and Lowell had .22 pistols and I had my .222 rifle. We spent all afternoon just having a great time catching plenty of fish, when we decided to quit fishing and go duck hunting. Billy and I were wasting a sandwich while sitting on the hand car. Lowell was shooting at some ducks when his gun jammed.

I had just stood up, ready to walk over to him to see if I could help him with his pistol when he turned around, pointing the pistol in my direction and fired. All of a sudden, I felt this burning sensation in my left leg in my thigh area. I was shot and when Lowell realized what had happened he started screaming and began to run toward town on the railroad tracks.

I calmly walked to the hand car to take my boot off to see

how bad it was, all the while listening to my friend Lowell screaming, "Oh no, I shot him! I shot Pops."

I wasn't hurt at all, and once I got my boot off I could tell it was just a minor flesh wound. Once Billy and I realized the bullet went right though the flesh and didn't hit any bone, he knew he would have to be the only one to push the hand car back into town because Lowell was still crying and literally useless to him. By the time we got into town Bill was soaking wet and winded from pushing the hand car the whole two miles by himself.

I was quite sore by the time we got into town and had to hobble up to the old retired army nurse's house not too far from the railroad tracks. She was concerned about powder burn and infection. She wanted to stick a cotton swab right through the wound, but I convinced her it was not necessary, mainly because I wasn't that close to Lowell when he shot me. She wrapped it up and I went home.

Well, three days later I was as good as new, and back to riding my bicycle and ready for more mischief.

My brother graduated from the eighth grade in 1953 and went to school in Holland, Michigan for two years. He had become close friends with the school principal who persuaded him to go to school in their home in Michigan. Bert was quite an artist and wanted to receive training in oil painting, and the principal helped him get an art scholarship. He became quite a celebrity during his two years there, becoming a quarterback on his school football team and lettering in track. His first year he broke four track records in the 100-yard dash, the 220-yard run, the 440, and 880-yard runs. The next year he went back and broke all his own records again and also made them state records as well.

A Wish Lost or Granted

I wish I may, I wish I might
Wish on a falling star tonight
Many stars have fallen in my lifetime,
And many wishes have been granted,
To see one seems to instill in us all,
A sense of well-being, a new beginning,
However, let us examine the true phenomenon
That minute flash of bright light means the end
Is near, as it burns up in our atmosphere,
And dies, never to ever sparkle again
But wait, another sparkling light emerges,
Bigger and brighter than the one that died,
A new star has just been born,
To replace the one I just wished on!

16

Dad's Most Amazing Talk

I'd like to relate to you just one of the many talks, or discussions, Dad had with my brother and me. This talk took place in Akwe in 1955, and I assure you that I didn't seriously think anything of it at the time, but as I remember the discussion now, I can truly see where Dad had a plan for our lives.

It was one of those beautiful, sunny afternoons in July, as the three of us returned from delivering fish to Dry Bay. Dad was driving the truck and we were almost home when we spotted a large brown bear just ahead of us, eating strawberries. Dad stopped the truck and took a few pictures, and told us boys to get out and stretch our legs for a while.

As he took pictures, he kept saying "Ah, beautiful! Come on, bear, look at me now. Good." Then he'd snap a picture. As he completed his picture taking, he took in the serene beauty of the area, all the while taking deep breaths of fresh air, saying "Ahhh, smell the fresh salty air, sons."

Then he stretched out his arms to emphasize his point as he pointed to the horizon saying, "Sons, take a good hard look around you, because someday this will be all yours. I want you to remember everything I taught you about fishing in this river because it has been good to us for the last five years, and if we take care of it, it will continue to nourish us for many years to come. I'm trying to emphasize an important point here that I want you boys to remember," he said as he looked back at the bear munching away, oblivious to us being in his domain.

Dad continued on, saying, "Take that bear for example. If that was a female with cubs, she wouldn't let us come this close to her without running off with her cubs because she would want to protect them from us, thinking we may harm them. It's the same way with people, sons, because this river will soon die out, and all because of greed.

"Sons, I have turned down many people from town (Yakutat) who want to become partners with me because they know this is a good producing river, and in the near future you too will be getting requests from your friends about being partners with you. Always remember what I have told you, sons, and when you do decide, I know your decision will be the right one.

"In other words, sons, you take from the land and the river only enough to sustain you. Never ever kill or waste anything for pleasure, or greed, because the land and the river will eventually die, never to produce berries or the fish again. Remember these words well, sons, because as you grow up, you'll find out later in life that if you live by the laws of nature and understand life, then you'll always be taken care of by the land and the sea.

"Sons, that wasn't what I wanted to talk to you about, but I hope you boys understand what I tell you because times are changing real fast. I want you boys to have a firm stake here on the Akwe River, and we have been writing to the Forest Service for the past two years now trying to get an allotment of 160 acres for our homestead, but there is a lot of paperwork involved and we have to prove that your mother's ancestors lived here and used the lands as their fishing site. Do you boys realize that if this goes through the Forest Service, we will practically own this river?

"Always remember, sons, I've always called this place God's country and it truly is, because if you work hard and believe in your convictions, good things will start happening because the Good Lord takes care of those that believe.

"Anyway, I want to build us a permanent home here on the timber side over there somewhere, about halfway up river. Hopefully, maybe by the time the next fishing season arrives, we may be able to build us a nice log cabin, huh?

"Well, sons, we'd better be moving on now. Your mother will have dinner ready for us, and you know how she is about being late," he said, as we all jumped back into the truck and headed for home.

Little did we know that this would be the last major "talk!' Dad would have with us. It really seemed to me as I look back on it now that the timing was just perfect, because he never had a chance to complete his dream.

The true love of a father's son and a promise made is certainly a legacy I want to keep.

A Promise Kept

I have no great legacy to pass on to my children
And I'm certainly not from the rich and famous
All I have is this true story Id like to tell you
About the dedicated love of a father's son
And a promise I made to Dad a long time ago
It was way back in '57, when he became quite ill
He was dying of cancer and knew his time was near
I was just seventeen when he called me to his bedside
He made me promise to take care of Mom after he left
For that Promised Land where all good people go
I didn't realize what a hard struggle it would be
It took many long years of comforting and caring
Mom literally went to pieces and took comfort in a bottle
'Cause she lost the only love she ever knew
And couldn't face the thought of going on without him
She tried to drink herself into a world of oblivion
'Til she realized she had to turn her life around
I was there for her and helped her fight the battle
She finally won the fight over the helpless boozing
And couldn't thank me enough for helping her
Even as she, too, lay dying of cancer and knew
That she would soon be meeting Dad
In that Promised Land, where all good people go.

17

Dad Dies

The following school year my brother and I were both attending high school at Mt. Edgecumbe High School in Sitka, Alaska.

About two weeks before school was out, my brother and I were called in to the school principal's office. We were told that Dad was dying of cancer and wanted to see us before he passed away. This came as a real shock to us because we never even knew Dad had been sick.

The very next day a bush pilot friend of ours from Yakutat landed his small plane on the ramp area below the school to pick up my brother and me.

The pilot, Butch Vent, was a close friend of the family and when we started barraging him with questions about Dad's condition, he couldn't, or wouldn't, elaborate at all. He did tell us that he had been visiting Dad almost every day and had seen him earlier that morning. He told us boys that Dad apparently had developed cancer quite some time ago, but never let anyone know he was sick until the pain got too bad for him.

Butch flew us to Juneau because Dad was at St. Ann's Hospital and I tell you, not one of us spoke a single word throughout that flight. My brother and I were devastated and were not mentally prepared to see Dad in such a sickly state. I don't need to tell you, but I wasn't looking forward to this meeting. Throughout the flight to Juneau, my mind kept flashing back to the "good ole days," when we were kids, wrestling around with Dad on the kitchen floor of our home in Yakutat.

I had always thought of Dad as being invincible and as tough as a bear.

I used to love it when he would rub his beard against our cheeks, almost making us cry, but we'd always be asking for more beard rubs.

Tears started flowing down my cheeks as I remembered that I never even told him flat out that I loved him since I was about seven or eight years old. That was about ten years ago, and I wondered if he really knew how much my brother and I worshipped him. As far as we were concerned, he was the king and we were his servants. Then I found myself thinking about how Mom might be taking all this. I know she loved Dad very much and I began to wonder what she would do if she lost him. I couldn't even imagine how she would endure such a tragedy!

My thoughts were interrupted as we landed at the Juneau airport and taxied to a stop as Butch Vent turned off the engine and told us that he would drive us to St. Ann's Hospital.

Mom was waiting for us at the entrance door of the hospital and after the hugs and tears she tried her best to prepare us mentally before we went in to see Dad. She told us that the doctors had given him about three to six weeks to live and that we should be strong and encouraging and not break down when we saw him. My brother and I kept our promise to Mom, but it certainly wasn't easy, looking at Dad, who was now just a shell of his former self.

We stayed for three days, and three weeks after we had returned to school at Mt. Edgecumbe, we received a phone call from Mom, saying Dad had passed away that morning.

After returning back to school at Mt. Edgecumbe, I found myself dabbling with poetry, apparently as an outlet for my innermost feelings. I wrote this poem for my dad after he passed away in May, 1957.

Wishes

I wished upon a falling star once upon a time
My wish came true, but it really wasn't mine
It was for you, Dad, that wish I wished that night.
You were so frail and weak that you could hardly speak.
But the voice I heard sounded like a mockingbird
On that fateful day in May when my dad had passed away.
Now whenever I look up in the sky at night
As promised I can always see with delight,
His face smiling down at me from Heaven above.

This may be very controversial, but it is truly my own personal religious belief.

I Believe

*I believe a master plan
has been laid down by a higher power.
You can call it God, Master of the Universe,
or whatever you like.
Our destiny on earth cannot be controlled by man.
It lies in the hands of a much greater power than ours.
The secrets of the universe and of mankind lie in wait.
It waits for our development as humans to be complete.
Some bits and pieces are just now slowly being implanted.
We're being programmed to absorb
the knowledge and understand.
I believe there is no real death here on earth for any of us,
We live in a spiritual life after our earthly bodies die.
A new and higher plan of life
means a new beginning for me,
When my heart stops pumping
the lifeblood through my veins.*

18

Summer without Dad

Mom had a male friend by the name of Johnny Lamb living with her during the summer of 1957, just months after Dad had passed away. The summer of 1957 was a year of adjusting for all three of us, without Dad around. It seemed like our family structure had broken down and both of us were left making our own decisions now.

Mom's friend Johnny Lamb was an excellent mechanic so he did all the major maintenance on the truck and our outboards.

It was decided that we would build a permanent home on the timber side of the Akwe River. We all chose a site about two and a half miles upriver and proceeded to build our permanent log cabin. Johnny Lamb didn't realize it, but Mom, my brother and I were completing a legacy of Dad's.

It took us all, working until dark each night, about three weeks to complete our new home. Mom's friend drew up the plans and marked the trees he wanted to cut, and my brother would cut them down with a chainsaw. I would cut the limbs off, then Mom and I would peel the bark off. We had kind of an assembly line going, each one of us being given certain tasks. Both Bert and Johnny Lamb did all the hauling of the logs, using a sophisticated system of come-alongs that would haul the logs to the actual site location. We finally moved into our newly built log cabin in late June with a festive baked salmon dinner and strawberry cream puffs for dessert!

Ever since I can remember, Dad used to show us boys how to locate a good place to set our nets and how to read the river flow.

I want to explain an incident that truly happened to me during our first opening. I had my three nets in my skiff heading downriver to set them out. I had no problem finding good locations to set the first two nets, but was really having a hard time trying to decide where to set the last one.

One of Dad's last statements to me before he passed away was to remember how he taught us where to set our nets.

He also told us that we would know if we made a set in the wrong spot because he would kick us in our rear end.

I finally picked a location, but was very undecided about whether it was a good location or not. I picked up my anchor and threw it on the sandy bank, but it seemed like it kept hitting a large rock or something. It kept bouncing off the sand and wouldn't dig in like it should. I walked along the shore, trying to get this anchor embedded in the sand, but it just wouldn't sink into the sand. I had a strange sensation and the hair on the back of my neck was standing straight up.

I finally had to move up river about fifty feet before the anchor finally embedded itself into the soft sand, and I felt that I had found a good location. It turned out that one net had the most fish each time I had picked up my nets. I honestly believe that my dad was with me that day, helping me through that ordeal.

Mom was taking it quite hard without Dad around, but she soon put the past behind her and used to tell us we were her only reason for living now. It seemed like we each needed our own privacy that summer—a time when we would each just go our separate ways to contemplate our thoughts. I spent a lot of time going upriver to explore the different river channels and to fish for rainbow and cutthroat trout. Bert used to take long walks along the ocean beach, sometimes staying all day, returning just before dark. Mom's only outlet was her drinking, or she would keep herself busy by smoking or drying salmon and canning them for her winter food supply.

I had tamed a family of squirrels that lived under a pile of alders that we had cut to make a trail through the heavy timber. Every morning we would awaken to the constant chatter of these squirrels looking for a handout. They had started getting used to me because I had been throwing them scraps of leftovers and then tying a piece of bacon rind to the end of my fishing pole line. I would cast out the bacon rind and they would grab it with their paws, chewing away as I would reel the line in, getting them right alongside of me.

Sometimes all three of us would be out by that pile, practically having all four of the squirrels eating out of our hands. We would spend hours at a time playing with those squirrels.

Since Bert graduated from high school, he had planned to live in Yakutat after the fishing season ended. However, I was going to be starting my junior year. We hardly made enough money to pay expenses by the time the coho season began so we were all hoping for a good run of cohos, or "silvers."

It was decided that I would get a moose for Mom's winter food supply. We would have it flown to Yakutat to be butchered and packaged and stored in a large freezer until after the fishing season ended. As soon as the moose season opened I went upriver early one morning, planning to go directly to a large open meadow that was our favorite location for spotting moose.

The upper Akwe River was a twisting, winding river which originated from a lake about eight miles upstream. Around almost every curve or bend in the river was an open area or meadow which is a natural habitat for moose.

The weather was overcast with a heavy mist, or fog, lying low to the ground, but the forecast called for the sun to come out, which would burn off the fog later in the day. I had only gone upstream about a half a mile when I spotted a large bull moose standing on the edge of the river bank, feeding on the willow shoots which always grew around the river's edge. As I approached, I soon realized he was too large, so I just watched as he trotted off into the underbrush. I wanted a nice young bull, not an older one, because the meat would be too tough.

As I continued my journey I saw two brown bears feasting on salmon on a sandbar. All around them were carcasses of salmon, now being picked clean by the ravens and crows, oblivious to my presence in their domain. As I rounded another bend in the river, there on the bank of the river was a nice two-year-old bull moose, just browsing in the willows.

I cut the engine and coasted to the bank, grabbing my .30 x .30 and, being as quiet as I could, anchored the skiff. I crouched down among the alders and began to slowly walk to the area where I last saw the bull, all the while listening for any noise.

There he was, not more than seventy-five yards in front of me, as I aimed for a spot just below the ear.

"Kra-ack!" went the sound, as the bull just dropped to the ground, not knowing what hit him. I immediately put another round in the chamber as I stood up and watched the bull for a few minutes for any movement. I saw no movement, so I started approaching him. I was about fifty feet away when I saw something out of the corner of my eye to the right.

Out of the brush comes this young cow moose, ready to charge me. I immediately started backing away as fast as I could, all the while keeping a close eye on the young cow, which was now snorting, its head bobbing up and down, and its front legs pawing at the ground.

I was about a hundred yards away, with my weapon ready, as the cow raised its head and stiffened, its whole body rippling with taut muscles as it started a slow trot toward me. I surprised myself by waving my arms and yelling at the young cow as it came toward me, advancing to about fifty feet, and then just stopped in its tracks. It turned around and trotted back to where the young bull lay, sniffing and pawing at it, apparently trying to get it to get up.

Believe me, I really felt bad for shooting what must have been the cow's mate, but at the time I never did see the cow at all. I was now in my skiff, watching and waiting for over a half hour before the cow finally trotted off into the timber. I didn't waste any time at all as I quartered the young bull, and within an hour I had the complete carcass in my skiff headed for home.

The moose was flown into Yakutat to be cut and packaged and kept in a freezer until Mom and Bert moved into town where it would be divided between the two of them. Mom also had about ten cases of smoked salmon and ten cases of canned salmon with about twenty gallon jars of dried salmon, all flown into town for storage.

The day finally came when I had to go back to school at Mt. Edgecumbe High School. I tried to persuade Mom and my brother to let me stay until the season ended, but Mom wouldn't hear of it, saying my education was more important than anything else right now. I really felt guilty though for having to leave just before the real coho run even started. We had such a poor sockeye season and hadn't even made any profit yet. I started to have my doubts about even wanting to finish high school, thinking only of helping my mom and brother make some money.

My brother really made me come to my senses though, because I was just starting my junior year and he reminded me of a track meet I was in just before school was out last year. He told me that high school was like running a mile relay, which takes four runners each running 220 yards four years of high school (each year being roughly nine months).

He reminded me of the time I was in a track meet last year

between Mt. Edgecumbe and Sitka High School. I was the second runner in this mile relay race, each of us running 220 yards. I was just passing this Sitka student when all of a sudden he just fell to the pavement, literally exhausted, scraping his face and hands as he made contact with the cement. Being the concerned citizen that I am, I actually stopped running and bent down to see if there was anything I could do for him. Not even aware that I had stopped until I could hear the shouts from the crowd saying don't stop, keep running—-which finally I did, and we still won the race.

My brother told me that I was having doubts and guilt feelings just like I did during that race, but I should not interrupt my schooling just because I felt I would be more helpful if I stayed to help them finish up the season. He went on to tell me that I had to finish that race to complete my education and not stop in the middle of my race for any reason.

I really have to credit my brother for encouraging me on like he did, because that thought stuck with me for the next two years, up to my graduation in May of 1959, and continues to this day.

How many times have you said, "I'll never do that again." The very next week you're out there doing it again. This advice never seems to sink in, huh?

Caught in a Storm

Life surely has its share of ups and downs
We're supposed to learn by our past mistakes.
We vow never to make those same mistakes again,
But we always do, time and time again.
Some continue this trend throughout their lifetime.
Life is like being tossed around at sea in your boat,
Caught in a sudden storm, far away from any safe port.
You dip and dive and toss and turn like a cork.
You flounder around, as if you're dead in the water.
At the mercy of Mother Nature in her finest hour.
Ever so slowly, you pound those waves mercilessly,
Heading for land, still way off in the distant horizon.
It's rougher than ever, as you wonder if you'll make it.
But you've done it many times before
and it will surely happen again.
Finally, scared, but safe, you reach port and tie up.
The first words out of your mouth are
"I'll never do that again."
Oh, you'll live to fish another day, but never in a storm
Until the next time, that is, until the next time.

19

Mom Works for Dr. Phillip Moore

Mom had been having a lot of problems with her left knee over the past summer. Her kneecap seemed to pop out of place at least three or four times a day and either my brother or I used to grab her ankle and pull down until it snapped back into place. Mom assured us she would have her knee taken care of after the fishing season so we didn't think too much of it at the time.

I was in school at Mt. Edgecumbe in January 1958 when I was paged in my dorm to go to the office to take a phone call. It was Mom saying she was in town to have her knee surgery and had landed a job as a housekeeper and cook for Dr. Phillip Moore, the same doctor who was to do her surgery. As far as I can remember that had been the first phone call I or my brother had ever received from our parents throughout our high school years, simply because that was how they were. We would probably receive a short note from Mom on our birthdays and again at Christmastime.

We each had a bank account at the school for our spending money and always had enough clothes to last us through the school year so we were pretty well set for the year. There were about twelve other kids from Yakutat at Mt. Edgecumbe also, so we would always hear the latest news from one of them.

Anyway, Mom had arranged to check me out over the weekends to be filled in about her upcoming knee surgery from Dr. Moore himself. I never mentioned this to anyone before, but for some reason I had a secret desire to become a doctor, even though I never ever seriously thought about the number of years of schooling it took to become a doctor.

Throughout my high school years I was never very serious about my schoolwork. I never had any real problems doing homework or anything like that, I did just enough to get by, and never was on the honor roll, and had about a C+ average in all my grades.

I was so happy for Mom because it seemed like she was really trying to get her life in order and this opportunity was certainly a step in the right direction.

I had heard earlier that Dr. Moore and his wife, Phyllis, lost their two teenage sons in a skiing accident in Sitka sometime just before Christmas. They apparently got caught in an avalanche while skiing and both had died.

The weekend finally arrived, and I was checked out from six P.M. Friday to 8 P.M. Sunday. I was told to take a cab to the Moore Clinic, where they lived. Their home was large and beautiful, with a large dining room and a sunken living room. It was a duplex, with living quarters upstairs and a complete doctor's clinic and exam room downstairs.

After the introductions, we sat down to a fine turkey dinner Mom had prepared. During the meal Dr. Moore filled me in on Mom's upcoming knee surgery. He explained that she had torn a ligament in her kneecap and fluid had built up. He would have to drain the fluid and repair the ligament, and hopefully she shouldn't have any further problems afterwards. She was scheduled for surgery on Wednesday of the following week.

After dinner, the four of us retired to the living room where Dr. Moore lit up his pipe, and began to tell us about the tragic loss of their two sons, just two months ago. With tears in our eyes after Dr. Moore finished telling us about his sons, he asked me how I felt about losing my dad the previous year. Both Mom and

I poured out our feelings of loss because neither of us were ever in a situation like this before, where we were asked how we really felt about Dad being gone from our lives. We must have talked for hours before having some of Mom's apple pie and then retiring for the night.

The next day, Saturday, I didn't see Dr. Moore until just before supper. Mom and I spent the afternoon shopping for clothes and talking about how happy she was, having a job and hoping she could stay away from drinking.

I had completely forgotten about wanting to become a doctor, but I guess Mom had mentioned it to Dr. Moore and his wife because I soon felt like I was being wined and dined and given expensive gifts for some reason other than just as a friend. About three months of the good life of fancy dinners and being checked out every weekend going on Dr. Moore's fancy thirty-six-foot yacht was becoming a bit too much for a boy from the sticks. Finally, one weekend in April, I was told by Dr. Moore that an upcoming event would be taking place at their home and I was to dress formal for the occasion. I thought the event had something to do with Mom because Dr. Moore had been trying to treat Mom for her alcoholism. She was supposed to be taking Antabuse but stopped taking it whenever she felt the urge to drink. The date finally arrived and I got the shock of my life. Mom had apparently started drinking the night before and never did show up to cook dinner so Phyllis Moore had to cook. Dr. Moore had invited two other couples to the dinner and to this day I cannot remember who they were, other than the fact that they were also doctors and their wives.

After dinner we retired to the living room and I assure you that I wasn't prepared for what happened next.

Dr. Moore lit up his pipe as he sat in his easy chair and began his speech.

"Son, I've called you here tonight because Phyllis and I have become quite attached to you and a matter of fact have come to love you as if you were our own son. We thought we would come right out and tell you we would like to adopt you as our son. We have also been aware that you have had an interest in becoming a doctor, and if that is so, we are more than prepared to send you through medical school at absolutely no cost to you in any way whatsoever. I know that all of this may seem as kind of a shock to you, but as I see it, time is of great importance right now. You will have to switch over to Sitka High School next spring in order to graduate with enough credits to qualify for pre-med school in Oregon."

He ended his speech with, "Well, son, I can see by your expression that you weren't expecting this so we'll give you a week to think it over. That's about it for now. You give us your answer next Saturday—okay?"

I don't think I slept for more than an hour that night as I lay in bed, tossing and turning, thinking about how easy it would be to say yes, but then thinking of a thousand excuses why I had to say no. I seriously considered the offer for the next two days, but only had to ask myself one question before I knew that I would turn the offer down. That one question I had to ask myself was, "Can you really do it?"

The following Saturday, after dinner, it was time for me to give a speech. Surprisingly, Mom had prepared a wonderful dinner, and made certain that I sat directly across from Dr. Moore, and as he lit up his pipe, I began to give my speech.

I looked Dr. Moore straight in the eyes as I started: "These past few months have been like a dream to me—a dream that is too good to be true, but this is the real world. In this real world I have come to love both of you as a father and mother, but I have had to ask myself a serious question over and over again, and that is this: Can I really become a doctor? Do I really have what it takes to become one?

"I can only answer that truthfully, and I'm being truthful to both of you when I say no. I would not want the burden on my shoulders if I said, 'Sure, I'll try' and then either flunk out or quit, but in my heart I know you will understand when I tell you that I don't have that feeling of commitment!

"Also, my dad's last words to me were, 'Always take care of your mother' and that is what I plan to do."

I closed my speech by saying how honored I was to have been given the opportunity of making my own decision and right or wrong, it was truly my decision and I hoped they won't ever hold a grudge against me for turning down their offer. I had tears in my eyes as I hugged Dr. Moore and his wife, Phyllis, and left their home for the last time.

Although we stayed close friends over the years, I truly believe Mom took it the hardest, because she soon turned to drinking quite heavily and lost her job with the Moores.

After school ended in May, I had to charter a small plane to fly Mom and me back to Yakutat because she wasn't sober enough to catch a commercial flight. I knew in my heart that Mom felt like she was more or less in my way of any opportunities on my part because of the situation with the Moores.

I tried my best to reassure her that I would always be there to take care of her and that whatever happened between me and the Moores had no bearing on her whatsoever. I reminded her of Dad's last wish, that I promised him I would always take care of her and now we had to start getting ready for the upcoming fishing season, which started in two weeks.

Nature in its natural state can change as fast as the different seasons come and go.

One with Nature

Black is the sky in the dark of the night
When the moon is unable to shine
No stars do I see to wish upon tonight
I'll save my wish for another time
The cool autumn wind rustles the trees
And somewhere an owl hoots goodnight
The smell of wood smoke permeates the air
The end of one season begins another
Soon, these hills will be covered with snow
How fast the changing seasons come and go
The sounds of nature are all around me
Peace and contentment fills my very soul
As I head back to my cabin in the woods.

20

Growing Up and Becoming a Man

We finally made it back to Yakutat and immediately arranged to move back out to Akwe for another year of fishing.

After clearing the cabin of the small rodents and squirrels that constantly seemed to be present everywhere, we washed all our bedding and settled in for another summer of fishing in God's country on the Akwe River.

The beautiful scenery never ceased to amaze me as I stood on the edge of the embankment overlooking the Akwe River, and the ocean beach beyond, the blue waves with the whitecaps crashing on the sandy beach about a mile away.

Bert and I were hanging our nets, putting the lead line and cork line onto the sockeye gear while Mom was preparing a big pot of boiled salmon. Mom had the radio on as we all listened to some easy listening music, and I began to find myself thinking about what a great life this was, doing something I truly loved; being a commercial fisherman.

I was jolted to my senses by the constant chattering of my family of squirrels, darting in and out of the pile of brush in front of me, apparently looking for a handout. There were now four young ones in this family, and it was as if they heard a dinner bell somewhere. After feeding them a bunch of scraps they all quieted down, maybe taking a short siesta.

As we ate our dinner that evening I told Mom that I was going up river tomorrow to catch some rainbow trout. This was early in June, and we hadn't had any rain for a long time so the river was really shallow. I planned on taking my skiff about a mile upriver to the sand dunes to walk a trail to the upper part of the Akwe River to a favorite trout hole of mine.

I was up early and packed a good lunch for my outing as I headed upriver. I was indeed content and began whistling some tunes as I made my way up river. I was making slow progress because the river was so shallow. I had to constantly tilt the outboard motor and skim over the shallows.

I watched an eagle descend from its perch on a tree branch not more than one hundred yards in front of me and swoop down to the river with its talons open, ready to strike a sockeye salmon wallowing in the shallows. I sat and watched in awe as the eagle caught its prey in a death grip and proceeded to return to the same tree branch to devour its fresh meat. As it landed it screeched its announcement to the other eagles in the area as if saying, "there's plenty more where this one came from."

I finally arrived at the sand dunes and anchored the skiff, gathering my stuff together for the mile walk to the heavy timber. The sand dunes is just an area on the timber side of the Akwe River where there must have been a glacier many, many years ago because it was just an area of sand dunes surrounded by heavy timber.

It was just now about six-thirty A.M. as I gathered my belongings, getting ready for my trek through the soft sand. A chill went up my spine as I heard the eerie, sad cry of a wolf off in the distance. It went "ahowoo-oo-h" and made the hair on the back of my neck stand straight up. I didn't think too much of it because it sounded like it was quite far away. However, I stopped to check my trusty .30x.30 making sure it was loaded and the safety was on.

This walk normally took about a half hour before entering the heavy timber. From there the trail, which was actually a bear trail, led to the bank of the upper part of the Akwe River (another ten- to fifteen-minute walk on the bear path). I hadn't gone more than a hundred yards when I sensed something, or felt something, watching me. I stopped and looked around me, all the while feeling certain that I was being watched by something, but not seeing anything.

I was beginning to get a little jittery, but trudged along in the soft sand, always keeping a close eye out for any movement all around me.

Suddenly, I noticed something dark moving along the alders about two hundred yards ahead of me. I froze in my tracks as the large, black wolf trotted toward me as if I weren't even there. I realized it didn't see me yet and the wind was blowing in the wrong direction for it to catch my scent so I figured I'd better scare him off.

I fired a round from my .30x.30 into the air and began to holler and wave my arms at the wolf. He jumped straight into the air about a foot off the ground and trotted off in the direction of the heavy timber. I'd seen many gray wolves before, but this was the first black wolf I had ever seen. I still don't know if it was the one that I sensed watching me, but I didn't stay around to find out, either. Before I entered the timber area I checked my .30x.30 to make certain I added another bullet into the chamber and had the safety on.

As I entered the wooded area, I began to cough and make as much noise as I could to scare off any bear that might be in the area because this path I was taking was actually a bear trail leading to the river. A squirrel started chattering as I trudged along the trail, apparently warning any other animals that were in the domain.

Soon the wooded area gave way to an open meadow about a quarter of a mile wide and at least a mile long. This open meadow was a favorite spot of mine to see a moose, and I have yet to be disappointed in not spotting at least one each time I've been there.

I was about halfway across the meadow when I turned and looked back to a cluster of willows that grew around the meadow. Sure enough, there to my right about five hundred yards away was a young bull moose feeding in the willows. I watched for a few minutes before continuing through the trail, which soon opened up on the edge of the upper Akwe River. I finally arrived at my destination.

This river was actually one of the clear-water tributaries that originated from a lake about eight miles upriver, emptying into the Akwe about two miles downstream. I've been to this same spot many times before, but each time I come here I am always amazed at the beautiful setting. The trail ends on a clay bend about eight feet high where the river takes a U-turn. I was standing on this bank at the bottom of the U where I could look at the upper part of the river about a hundred yards, and to the lower part of the river on my right I could also see about a hundred yards downriver before it went around another bend. Across the river, about seventy-five feet away, was a gravel bar that followed the curve of the river

Off to my right was a large spruce tree that fell across the river, now dangling at about a forty-five-degree angle, with only its branches touching the water. The whole root system of the tree had gouged out a large hole about twenty feet in diameter providing a natural pool now filled with minnows or fingerlings. The water was a rusty brown color with a hint of gold as the bright sun shone down over the rippling current of the natural flow of the river.

It was just now about nine A.M. as I began to get myself settled in for a good time of fishing. I tied my knapsack to a tree limb directly behind me as I rested my .30x30 against the base of the same tree as I began to get my fishing pole ready for action.

I put a cube of salmon on my hook and cast out into the river, letting the current carry the hook downstream into the deep hole just under the fallen tree to my right. Within half an hour I had landed eight nice large rainbow trout, more than enough for a nice breakfast for the three of us.

I decided I'd caught enough, so I lashed my trout to a line and left them in a pool under the trunk of the tree just below me and to my right. I was beginning to get hungry so I decided to eat a sandwich and have some coffee from my thermos. I leaned against the base of the tree behind me and began to eat my sandwich. I watched a kingfisher dive into the river and come up with a small fingerling in its mouth as it flew off to a small tree nearby. And around me were the sounds of a variety of different birds calling to each other.

Across the river along the clay bank, I watched a couple of otters playing in the shallows, sliding down the clay bank like a couple of kids, repeating the process over and over again. I finished my lunch and was content to just relax for a while before I started exploring the area further. I must have dozed off because I awoke to the low grunting sound of a large brown bear already in the tidal pool, munching on my trout. I instinctively grabbed my .30x.30 and my knapsack as I spun around the tree I was leaning against. Apparently, the bear didn't even see or smell me, because it continued to eat my trout as I beat a hasty retreat out of there as fast as my legs could go. I didn't stop once until I came out of the heavy timber at the sand dunes.

Mom and my brother didn't believe my story at all until the following weekend when we all went upriver for more trout fishing and a picnic. We stopped at the spot where I was fishing and sure enough the bear tracks were still there in the soft clay, along, with nothing but bones left of my trout. I found my fishing pole and put it into the skiff as we continued our trip further up river.

I had one other close encounter with a bear one night as I

left the cabin, walking the short distance of about twenty yards to the top of the bank on my way back to tend to my nets. At the top of the bank, the trail goes down the seventy-five-foot sandy embankment at about a forty-five-degree angle to the river's edge. It was about two A.M. on an overcast night in September and it was pitch black out. I was still attaching my headlight strap to my forehead as I approached the top of the bank so the light wasn't even on yet, and I didn't make any noise at all.

Just as I was about to take my first step off the bank I turned my flashlight on and not more than five feet in front of me this large bear reared up on its hind legs and let out a growl, as I screamed and did an immediate about-face and ran back to the cabin as fast as I could. I don't know who was more afraid, me or the bear, because the next day I could see where the bear actually rolled partway down the bank, finally ambling off downriver along the sandy beach by the river's edge.

As far as I can remember I have never been afraid of being around animals such as bear or moose in the wild, probably because I grew up being around them all my life.

Bees and spiders, however are a different story, and for some reason I am truly afraid of them.

My dad had always taught us boys that all animals can sense fear in humans so that if you do encounter one in the woods you should never panic or run from them. I have seen several instances where I have found this advice to be so true and I honestly believe that I am still here today because I heeded that advice.

I was picking blueberries one time in the heavy timber area not too far from our cabin, when I came out onto a semi-open area and encountered the foul smell of a bear that must have been not more than twenty feet ahead of me. The smell of the bear can only be described as rank; it reminded me of the fresh smell of skunk cabbage, or recently upturned wet moss which has a very rank smell.

I had forgotten one of my own rules about making a lot of noise when you're in the woods, because I had found a large patch of those yellow salmon berries that are so sweet and tasty; I was too content with just filling my stomach. When I encountered the smell I immediately froze in my tracks and listened for any noise in the underbrush around me as I backed off about ten steps and made a wide semi-circle around the area. Only after I had gone around the bear did I start to whistle and make all kinds of racket. I could hear the crackling in the brush and twigs as I scared the bear away from the area.

In Alaska I think most people will agree that the grizzly bear is probably the most feared animal to encounter. However, I believe that pound for pound the wolverine is by far the fiercest animal in Alaska. Though small in stature, they are the meanest and one of the smartest animals I have ever encountered, about the same size as an overgrown otter, but that is where the similarities end. The wolverine has short, stubby legs with long short claws that can disembowel a bear with just one swipe. Their bloodshot eyes have the look of the devil himself, and their razor-sharp teeth are made for tearing or ripping flesh.

I have seen the results of what one did to our smokehouse in Dry Bay several years ago. Mom had smoked two hindquarters of moose that were hanging on racks in our smokehouse, which was built out of sturdy four-inch-diameter poles covered over with planks, all nailed up solid and tight. The door had three large latch hinges and was locked with a large sliding-door latch.

A wolverine literally tore the front door off its hinges and carried those two hindquarters about one thousand yards away from the smokehouse, where we found nothing but the scattered remains of some bones the following day. Dad had finally shot it after tying some meat to a tree and sitting up for four nights before it finally came by and tried to get at the meat.

I had been having problems with bears tearing up my nets and eating many of the fish. I had this one particular net that was always filled with fish, but for the past week was practically ripped into pieces because a bear had been tearing the web, getting at the salmon. I decided I would take matters into my own hands and sit and wait for the bear and shoot it because it was costing me money.

I tied my skiff to the end of my net and decided to sit and wait for the bear to come by. I didn't have to wait too long because I soon felt a tug on the corkline as I turned my headlamp on and shone my light directly into the bear's eyes. He was not more than twenty feet away from me, about five feet offshore in the water, holding the cork line up over his head, looking for salmon in the meshes.

I grabbed my 30-06 and fired a round directly into his right shoulder, hoping I'd drop him with one shot through the heart but I had no such luck. I heard the most blood-curdling growl I have ever heard, as the bear started to climb the sandy embankment up to the heavy timber at the top of the bank.

I watched and waited for about fifteen minutes before I decided I had to go after the bear, knowing that he was wounded quite badly.

I walked downstream a bit before I started the slow climb up the sandy bank up to the heavy timber at the top of the bank. As scared as I was, I knew I had to kill the bear and not let it roam around wounded and get away from me. I crawled through the alders and brush until I could hear the bear growling and could see him rolling around on his back, trying to cover himself with leaves and moss, apparently preparing himself to die.

I crawled to within fifty feet and stood behind a large spruce tree as I fired three more rounds into him before I knew he was really dead, as he finally stopped moving. I went straight home, but went back the next day to cover the bear with branches to give him a decent burial.

When the season finally ended I cleared about $9,000, so the effort and hard work was well worth it.

My brother moved to Sitka and took a job with the U.S. Public Health Service at Mt. Edgecumbe, Alaska.

I spent a few weeks in Yakutat after the fishing season trying to figure out what I wanted to do with myself.

Retaliation for man's neglect and blindness will soon permeate
the world.

Mother Earth

Nature in its natural state is both beautiful and frightening.
We are always fascinated by the world's natural beauty.
In our parks we take pictures for posterity and our families
Because we know all too well that, in time, it will cease to be.
The sights and sounds of the world's changing seasons
come and go.
The thought of snowflakes
brings memories of winter and Christmas.
The warm sun and stars
remind me of the long warm summer months.
But forest fires, floods, tornadoes
hurricanes and earthquakes are devastating.
They are reminders of Mother Earth
retaliating at mankind's destruction.
We are drastically depleting all of earth's natural resources.
The minerals, the oil, the forests and even animals
are now endangered.
We're polluting our oceans and our own atmosphere is choking us.
I believe it's not too late to undo the damage we've already done.
For starters, a global educational process must be put in place.
We must be led to believe the Earth is just like a living organism
And stop taking the life-blood from her,
but learn to give her a transfusion.
After all, we're only here for such a short while and,
It's the least we can do
to preserve the world for generations to come.

21

Earthquake

The fishing season of 1958 was more or less a repeat of 1957, except we had more excitement than we had bargained for. I personally believe the poor fishing season had a lot to do with the earthquake in the Yakutat area that year.

It was July 9, 1958, at approximately seven P.M.

Mom and my brother, Bert, were playing a game of cribbage and I was lying on my bunk reading a pocketbook. The radio was on, as we were getting ready to listen to the news. We all stopped whatever we were doing and just stared at each other as we heard the sound.

It started out as a low, rumbling sound followed by a slow shaking movement of the ground, building up to a hard-jolting movement so intense it knocked pots and pans off the shelves and our radio fell into a bucket of water. We all glanced at each other with puzzled looks when someone shouted, "Earthquake!"

All three of us made a beeline for the door of the cabin, thinking a tree might topple over onto the roof of the cabin. As we exited the cabin the sound of the trees swaying back and forth was so loud it was as if a high wind was blowing, but there was no wind at all. We couldn't even stand upright because the ground was swaying as if the ground was water and it had this kind of rippling wave motion.

I crawled to the embankment hoping that our truck was okay. After assuring Mom and Bert the truck was okay, we decided we'd better check with the Mortenson family up the river from us because they had a two-way radio. By now the ground had stopped shaking and we were all able to stand as we went back to the cabin to survey the damage. Other than the radio falling into a bucket of water and a few cups and some pots and pans scattered around the floor, there didn't seem to be any major damage at all.

We just grabbed our jackets and as we went back outside, I picked the radio up out of the bucket of water and set it on a shelf, hoping that it wasn't permanently damaged.

The Mortensons were a family from Petersburg, Alaska who had fished in the Akwe River for years. Their cabin was about two and a half miles upriver, about a half-hour drive from where we were located. We hurriedly proceeded down the sandy trail to our skiff to go across the river to our truck.

As we got into our skiff, we all noticed a small bear about halfway across the river on the flats trying to come across the river, but getting stuck in quicksand. It would rear up on its legs and stretch on its front paws until its hind legs would come loose of the sticky, gooey mud and start the whole process all over again. Bert was having problems with the outboard motor so I started rowing across the river, all the time watching that bear struggling, but making some headway.

By now it had only been a few minutes since the ground had stopped shaking and we certainly didn't know what to expect next. We were about a hundred yards offshore when we heard this kind of gurgling, bubbling sound. The water was disappearing from the river! Like a giant sponge, the sand and sediment had drained the river completely dry, but only for a few seconds. As fast as it drained, the water started coming back up again, only this time it had a thick foam on top that smelled like something awful, like rotten eggs! As the water came back again I started rowing toward our truck as fast as my arms could go.

I honestly thought we would see a giant tidal wave next coming in from the ocean side, but it never happened. I don't need to tell you how scared we all were as we finally reached our truck and started the two-and-a-half-mile drive to the Mortensons' camp.

As we drove along our path we had to make several detours because there were several deep crevasses and cracks in the earth's crust. We still made the trip in record time though, not knowing what we'd find.

As we approached the Mortensons' cabin, they were all outside surveying the damage to their property. Their outhouse was toppled over and there were several deep, wide crevasses in front of their cabin that ran several hundred yards. Their front door was jammed stuck, halfway open but otherwise there was no major damage.

As we greeted each other, we heard a small plane approaching from the direction of Yakutat. Soon the plane was overhead as Mr. Clint Mortenson made radio contact with the pilot, Mr. Butch Vent, a local bush pilot, sent out to check on us. After assuring him we were all fine, he proceeded to Dry Bay to check on other fishermen there.

There were severe aftershocks for the next few days and I assure you no one slept well for about a week. We heard the devastating news about the three deaths in Yakutat when a portion of Khantaak Island sank to the ocean floor while three people were picking strawberries on the island. Khantaak Island is a long curved island that borders the entrance to Yakutat harbor, just off Ocean Cape.

Three close and dear friends of ours were picking strawberries on the island at the time the earthquake struck. A large portion of the island just broke off and sank to the ocean floor below. Nothing was ever found of the sixteen-foot skiff, nor their bodies as the island rose into the air about ten to twenty feet, then just sank to the ocean floor.

Another couple had just left the island a few minutes before this happened. The twenty-foot wave that was caused by the sinking of the island washed them high and dry onto the sandy beach of the old village as they rode the crest of the wave about a mile or so.

We had heard the epicenter of the quake was some one hundred miles or so offshore from Litulia Bay along the continental shelf. It was reported that the earthquake created the highest seiche or splash wave ever recorded. The quake registered a 7.9 on the Richter Scale, strong enough to influence the entire Yakutat area. It was said that if the area it impacted were of any population size, it would have caused much more major damage.

A landslide in Litulia Bay, which contained about forty million cubic yards of rock, plunged into Gilbert Inlet at the head of the bay, causing a gigantic splash that sent a wave 1,740 feet up the opposite side of the mountainside, sweeping trees and soil down to bedrock. A total of four square miles of forest was destroyed.

The wave swept back up the length of the bay and then swept back out to sea. A fishing boat anchored in Litulia Bay was washed out to sea with the wave. There were two crew members on it. They were all lost. Another vessel was carried over the spit of land. It sunk, but the crew was saved. A third boat survived the impact of the quake and resulting wave.

For weeks afterward there were logs from Litulia Bay washing up onto the beaches all up and down from Litulia Bay to Ocean Cape. They were stacked like cordwood, stripped clean of all bark and branches.

We take so much in life for granted—Why not request a blessing for all our beds?

Bless This Bed

I've spent a lifetime in this bed of mine
Many aches and pains have come and gone
This feathered-down has soothed them all
But now that it's old, I've got a hole
When I awake each morning now
Feathers fly, and I begin to sneeze
Lord, I'd like to ask you to please
Bless this feathered bed of mine
This bed means all the world to me
I'm old and tired now, and feel it's time
To rest my soul in this old bed of mine
But before I do, I'd sure like you to
Bless this holy bed of mine.

22

Marrying, Having Children, and Losing My Leg

After that summer, I really didn't know what I wanted to do so I planned to visit my brother in Sitka for a while before making any major decisions.

With no real plans and about $8,500 in my pockets, I left for Sitka, supposedly for just a few days to visit my brother. About two weeks later I fell in love, and eventually took a job at the Mt. Edgecumbe Hospital as a janitor. To make a long story short, I married Peggy Krukoff of St. Paul Island in Yakutat, Alaska on January 30, 1960, where we made our home.

I took a job with the Federal Aviation Agency working as a maintenance person and painter until June of 1961. My first son was born on November 14, 1960, and I was the proudest dad in all of Yakutat. I was passing out cigars for a whole week after he was born. By February of 1961, I had two sons, the youngest being just two months old when we moved to Los Angeles, California.

I had signed up for vocational training through the Bureau of Indian Affairs and selected a course of training as T.V. technician as my primary course and a nine-month arc-welding course as an alternate selection.

Apparently, students were given an option of changing courses within the first six months of training if they were flunking out of their primary course of training. This worked out great for me because I had never been out of Alaska, and being raised in the "sticks" and then all of a sudden finding myself going to school right in downtown Los Angeles was a bit much.

The first three months of schooling were the toughest months of my entire life. I had homework every night and I wasn't catching on to the math or the formulas used in the electronics industry. I knew that if I continued this course, I would probably flunk the quarterly test, which was coming in about two weeks, so I requested to transfer out of the T.V. Technician course and started a welding course.

The switch was approved and I really enjoyed welding. I studied really hard and became a certified pipe welder after nine months of training. The school was located in Southgate, California, a small suburb outside Los Angeles, and we didn't know at the time, but we were not far from Disneyland and Knots Berry Farm.

Being true Alaskans right out of the bush, we never visited Hollywood, even though we lived in an apartment on a hill overlooking Hollywood, California and could clearly see the large sign on the hillside below us. We lived two blocks from the Queen of Angels Hospital.

We were having a tough time just trying to exist on our weekly allotment from the Bureau of Indian Affairs so I decided I needed to find a job as soon as possible. I was three months away from completing my welding course and was doing just great and loved it, too.

We decided we would move back to civilization after completing my training, so I wrote a letter to the Alaska Lumber and Pulp Company in Sitka, explaining my qualifications and training as a welder and asked for a job.

In order for the Bureau of Indian Affairs to pay for our move back to Alaska, I had to have a "notice of hire" letter from my employer as proof of a job. I graduated from Allied Welding

School in December 1963, moved to Sitka, Alaska in January and started working at the pulp mill in Sitka in February 1963. I was hired as a laborer in the warehouse until a position as a welder became available. We were loading Japanese ships with wet sheets of pulp paper (blotting sheet size) which were to be made into rayon in Japan.

Things were looking good for us as a family and my wife was four months' pregnant when I finally started working. I had been working for approximately six weeks and was looking forward to Friday, April 12, because I had applied for a loan through the credit union and was anxiously awaiting their decision.

The scene is Sitka, Alaska, at the Alaska Lumber & Pulp Company Mill where I was working. It was Friday, April 12, 1963, at approximately 11:30 a.m. I was twenty-three years old working in the warehouse picking the four by four blocks out from under the pallets and stacking them as the forklift operator took the pallets of wet paper out to the loading dock. I had bent down to pick up two four by four blocks as the forklift operator started backing away, still raising his load.

Someone shouted, "Look out!" just as I was bending down. As I stood and glanced up I could see two top bales had slipped off and were falling directly toward my head. I remember trying to move out of the way, but felt like I was moving in slow motion.

I was struck on my left shoulder by one corner of the bale of wet paper. As the impact knocked me to the floor, the other corner had broken the tibia bone of my left leg about eight inches below the knee and shoved it right through the sole of my steel-toed boot. The bale finally came to rest about a foot away to the left of me, but not before breaking my ankle while lying flat on my back. I felt the concussion as I hit the concrete floor. My hard hat rolled to the side. I tried raising my head to sit up, but felt myself blacking out and went into immediate shock. I didn't feel any pain at all, just numbness throughout my whole body. I kept trying to sit up to look at my leg, but was immediately pushed back down by the first person to come to my aid. I remember being told that I would be all right and that I should he still.

It wasn't too long before there were about ten or more people gathered around trying to comfort me. I knew I was hurt pretty badly because I could hear their comments as someone put a blanket over me.

One said, "Oh, God," and another said, "Oh, man! His leg is gone!"

By now about fifteen minutes had elapsed and I still felt no real pain, but was feeling ice cold. My teeth were actually chattering as I heard the nurse say "We've got to get his boot off!"

I heard someone else say, "Anybody got a knife? These scissors can't cut anything!"

I could hear them tearing my pant leg and heard the blood pour out of my boot when they finally cut it off of my foot.

It seemed like an eternity, but I was hoisted up onto a stretcher and put into an ambulance. On the way to the hospital, the nurse gave me a shot for the pain. I could hear the wail of the siren, which seemed way off in the distance. I seemed to drift off into a deep, semi-conscious state and can remember this dream I had on the way to the hospital. I can recall the experience in such detail and with such vivid colors. I can still see the images in my mind as I apparently had this near-death experience.

"Black are the clouds in the darkest of nights." The shadow of death was looming near. An eerie silence settled into my brain. All my senses seemed to ebb away. I thrashed and moaned to fight the pain. All was in vain, to no avail, death beckoned me. Suddenly, I saw a bright light ahead. I felt as if I was floating in a tunnel somewhere. A feeling of peace and contentment overwhelmed me. As I traveled to the light, someone familiar was there at the end of the tunnel. He was beckoning me closer and closer, but before I arrived, I realized I was alive because I knew that "someone" was my Maker. As I started to awake, I was suddenly aware that I was in an ambulance somewhere and then I remembered why I was here.

Would you believe that as we pulled into the driveway of the Sitka Community Hospital emergency room, the doctor on duty was Dr. Phillip Moore? My mother worked for Dr. Moore from the fall of 1958 until May of 1959, as a housekeeper and cook. Dr. Moore and his wife, Phyllis, lost two sons in a skiing accident in Sitka during the winter of 1957. They were still grieving over their loss when my mother and I came into their lives. I was going to school at Mt. Edgecumbe at the time and was spending almost every evening visiting my mother. I began spending a lot of time with Dr. Moore. We became very close friends during that winter. I guess Dr. Moore became close, a father figure to me. The same doctor that wanted to adopt me in 1958 was now telling me that he would try to save my leg.

"Pops, I'm so sorry this happened to you," Dr. Moore said while the ambulance attendants wheeled me into the emergency room. They read off my vital signs to Dr. Moore and the nurse on duty.

Soon, I was moved from the gurney to an emergency room bed where I was being prodded and poked with needles. Then I heard Dr. Moore's voice again.

"I'm going to be very straight with you, Pops. You're in a very bad way. I'll do my best to save your leg, but I want you to know that we may have to amputate because it may be too shattered."

I barely remember telling Dr. Moore to just do whatever he had to do and I'd worry about it later. All I remember after that was darkness.

The next day, I awoke to Dr. Moore's voice saying, "Pops, time to wake up now. Your family is here to see you."

It seemed like the room was foggy as I tried to focus my eyes.

After a minute or so my vision became quite clear as I saw Dr. Moore leave the room. I glanced around the room and saw my wife, Peggy, and my two sons, Walter Jr. and Richard, sitting next to my bed. Peggy was crying quietly to herself, trying not to upset the boys.

Reality finally hit me like a ton of bricks as I lifted my head to look at my left leg. I knew it was amputated because my stump was propped up on a couple of pillows. As I wiggled the toes of my right leg, I compared the length between the two.

I barely remember throwing the covers off my stump and screaming, "Oh, no! Why me?"

In the next instance, it was as if I was watching a movie of my life flashing before me. I saw visions of myself running, jumping and doing everything a normal person with two legs would do. This vision of my life and the hysterical antics on my part lasted about a minute, but seemed like an eternity. As soon as the shock was over, I remember hearing a voice within me telling me to "Knock it off! You're lucky to be alive!" I remembered the accident and told myself I was definitely a lucky person. I made up my mind right then and there that I would never feel sorry for myself and would make the best of my life with whatever I had to offer.

The first two weeks after the accident were like a dream to me. I had visitors of all kinds. Some just wanted to convey their best wishes on my road to recovery and some were lawyers wanting me to sign some kind of paper on the dotted line.

I finally had to screen my visitors to see if I actually wanted to see certain individuals. I also contacted a lawyer friend of mine to represent me in order to refer anyone who wanted me to sign papers. I was covered under Workman's Compensation and started receiving checks every two weeks. It wasn't enough to cover the rent and food for my family so my wife, Peggy, who was a licensed practical nurse, had to go back to work at Mt.

Edgecumbe Hospital full time.

Exactly six weeks after my amputation, I was in Seattle being fitted for a prosthesis. This was when I received my indoctrination into the real world of what I like to call us "disadvantaged" people.

We all seem to forget about other people until something tragic happens to us and we become disadvantaged in some way ourselves. It took a serious accident and near-death experience before I realized how much I had been taking my life for granted.

Three hours after I arrived at Lunberg's Orthotics and Prosthetics in Seattle, Washington, I saw about twenty or thirty people worse off than me and it made me realize how lucky I really was. From that day on, I never considered myself handicapped at all, just a little disadvantaged.

I spent three of the longest, most agonizing weeks of my entire life being fitted with this piece of wood that would eventually be a permanent part of me until the day I die. It would be something I would have to rely on for walking for the rest of my life. Things went quite well for me mainly because my mind was in the right place. I was determined to make this piece of wood work for me the way it was supposed to. Finally, I received my completed prosthesis and was ready to tackle the world again.

I soon returned home to Sitka, still using a cane for support. Every day that went by, my walking improved, and I was soon walking without the support of a cane. I went through all the normal "phantom pains" and the cramps that all amputees experience. Let me try to explain the sensation: Have you ever had a cramp in your big toe where your big toe overlaps your second toe and cramps in that position? I was having a lot of those types of sensations. These are all normal sensations called "phantom pains" for an amputee because all of your nerve endings are still sending out signals to your brain.

Another sensation is where one of your toes itches so badly

that you can't get your shoe off fast enough to scratch that area. In my case though, I would take my prosthesis off and have to scratch an area on the end of my stump to relieve the itch. These sensations, although frustrating and nerve-wracking for the individual, do eventually go away. You really have to retrain your brain to ignore those signals though or otherwise you will be using those muscles and moving your toes, etc. trying to relieve the itch that way rather than re-training your brain to ignore those signals.

It was ten weeks after my accident when my lawyer called me into his office for an update on my case. Under Alaska law, all employees give up their right to sue the pulp mill in case of an accident and you have to accept Workmen's Compensation instead. This was one of the conditions of employment and was included in one of the forms each employee signed prior to being hired.

In 1963, under Workman's Compensation Law, the maximum payment for a below-the-knee amputation was $8,700. To make a long story short, after lawyer fees and expenses I ended up with a lump sum of $6,500. The only other agreement added to the settlement was that I was covered for any future medical problems pertaining to my amputation, all transportation costs and expenses to Seattle. Firemen's Fund Insurance Company would pay for all costs for my type of prosthesis for the rest of my life.

After contacting several lawyers regarding this settlement, I finally accepted the money and made plans to move back home to Yakutat, Alaska to be around my family and friends. I had to readjust my life and learn to walk with a prosthesis that would be a part of me for the rest of my life.

Positive thoughts and contentment of oneself through mind, body and soul, is true peace indeed.

Personal Peace

Being content with one's mind, body and soul
To attain it though is certainly not an easy task
But, Oh, what a wonderful blessing it can be
Negative thoughts and deeds must be all cast out.
Attitudes toward other people may need adjustment
We must teach ourselves to think good positive thoughts
We are limited only by our fear of not even trying
To work hard and achieve our future goals and dreams
And take good care of our bodies by staying healthy
And in the mirror of life we must love ourselves as one.
For me, it's a kind of spiritual awareness, or feeling I have
And, in my opinion, I am at peace. with myself, at last.

23

Business Adventure

I mentioned previously about how I saw visions of myself running and all that after I woke up and saw that my leg was actually amputated. I must tell you that I was now reliving those same visions, only this time with my prosthesis—trying to run with this ridiculous kind of skipping, hopping movement, wondering why I couldn't run like a normal person—even with the prosthesis. I seemed to feel that everyone or anyone that saw me in a supermarket or wherever knew that I was wearing a prosthesis, and to this day as I am writing this, I cannot seem to put that feeling out of my mind—so much so that I become nervous and sweaty whenever I am in a public place around a lot of people. This feeling, in my opinion, is my biggest downfall because as hard as I have tried to ignore my inner feelings, it is always uppermost in my mind—and I can't shake it for any reason.

I moved back home to Yakutat to sort of run away from the world and hide I guess. Well, it didn't take me long to realize that my home town was still just a small village and all my friends were now married and having children of their own or moving away to the larger cities to find work. I had been hibernating long enough and decided to start looking for work and became a true tax-paying citizen of the community.

It was the first part of 1964 and Yakutat seemed to be experiencing a kind of economic boom in housing and construction in the area. There was a construction crew building a road all the way to the Situk River (ten miles out of town) and I was informed that the road would continue all the way to the Alsek River. There were also some new homes being built by HUD (Housing and Urban Development). The city was just completing a water-storage facility large enough to have running water in all the homes within a year. I began to take a good hard look at my community and made several observations. There was no place for anyone in the community to go and get a hamburger and fries, or a milkshake, or a soft drink. This town needed to have a small café!

I had remembered the years I spent growing up as a child with no place to get an ice cream cone—and I really felt that this was what I wanted to do for the younger generation of children in Yakutat and maybe I could make a few dollars at the same time.

I had obtained a small business loan in the amount of $6,500 and with about $3,500 left over from my settlement money, I began making arrangements to order equipment. I rented the building next door to our house and completely remodeled it from the inside out, doing all the work myself—building my own booths and counter and purchasing all of my equipment out of Seattle, brand new.

I ordered a soft-serve ice cream machine, a deep fryer and grill, three-flavor juice dispenser, a Rock-ola jukebox, two refrigerators and a large freezer, along with all the other necessities like napkin dispensers, salt and pepper shakers, etc.

It was March of 1964, and I planned for a completion date of March first, with a big grand-opening celebration. I named my café "Pop's Café," after my nickname and thought at the time that I was sitting on top of the world!

I found out real fast why no one else ever opened a café before, because I had to charge an arm and a leg for a hamburger and fries. Everything had to be air freighted in from Seattle. My menu was simple, but adequate—serving hamburgers or cheeseburgers and fries, soft ice cream cones, milk shakes, three different flavors of soft drinks, floats, sundaes, pies or doughnuts which I made myself after obtaining a franchise to use Hole-N-One donut mix.

My children practically lived in my café during that first summer and winter because I was always there myself, cleaning up or making a batch of fresh donuts to sell the following day. Business was great on weekends, but during the week when everyone was out fishing I was just barely making expenses. I was chief cook and dishwasher for the first month, but finally hired a full-time cook and part-time dishwasher if I was ever going to get some rest myself.

Being the workaholic that I am, I soon became the deputy magistrate for the city of Yakutat, hired by District Judge Schultz of Juneau, Alaska. I also was the sanitation engineer for the city of Yakutat, taking care of the water-treatment plant and hooking people or households up to the city water system.

With all these jobs and the café to operate, I soon found that I was never ever home except to sleep and hardly ever spent any time with my wife because I was either at my café or at work somewhere. My wife was an LPN (Licensed Practical Nurse) and became a community health aide, spending a lot of her time with the Coast Guard medic whenever any medical problems arose or anyone had gotten sick.

Without going into all the details I will just say that because I was hardly ever home my marriage was soon falling apart. I had been hearing rumors about my wife and the Coast Guard medic.

I operated my café from May 1, 1964, through the fall of 1965, and kept my other jobs as well. I apparently thought that success and hard work would somehow improve my marriage relationship. One day I had just had it I guess, because I barely remember going to the store and buying this padlock, which I put on the front door of my café and told my wife that I was moving back to Sitka where I would go back to work at the Pulp Mill.

I had paid off the small business loan and everything in the café was paid for. So without looking back once I put the padlock on my café and just threw away about $12,000 in equipment.

Keep a smile on your face and a warm place in your heart and you'll do just fine.

Sound Advice

I was raised off the tremendous bounty
of the land and the sea,
And learned to appreciate the simpler things of life.
I realized something very important in life a long time ago,
Life is really too short
to dwell on the negative side of things.
We all must be positive in both our thoughts and our deeds.
We can all use an attitude adjustment every now and then,
And look at our reflection in the mirror of life.
Are we really happy and content with our lives?
We can all better ourselves and those around us,
Each in our own way, and a little bit at a time.
As for me, I'm finally happy and content with my life,
My positive outlook spreads out to those around me,
I believe people can sense the good in that,
and treat me in kind.
But I have always been a believer in the old saying
"It is never too late to teach an old dog new tricks"
Though some of life's best punches may be knockout blows,
Get up before the ten count, and the bell,
and come out swinging.
Keep a smile on your face and a warm place
In your heart and you'll do just fine.

24

Move Back to Sitka

After moving back to Sitka and finding an apartment, I had no problem getting hired on at the Pulp Mill in Sitka. Within a week my wife and kids moved down with me; however, our marriage was never the same. She went back to work at Mt. Edgecumbe Hospital as a practical nurse and I spent so much time in the Sitka Community Hospital because of stump problems for the next two years; it seemed I was doomed to stay on crutches for the rest of my life.

I found out that my real problems were with the fitting of my prosthesis, and my stubbornness. Being so anxious to get back to work, I didn't know the difference between the pain of a bad fitting and the normal feeling of wearing a prosthesis. I had developed a bad infection on the end of my stump that just wouldn't heal until I stayed completely off my prosthesis for six months! My stump finally healed and I was able to obtain a good fitting on my prosthesis because I now knew the difference between pain and comfort, if that makes any sense.

By this time, though, the Pulp Mill was reluctant to take me back and suggested I seek employment elsewhere because maybe my stump problems were psychological or something to that effect.

So I took their advice and drew unemployment for about a year. Finally in May of 1967, 1 took a job with Arrowhead Transfer Company in Sitka as an air freight agent when Alaska Airlines made their debut in Southeast Alaska.

In 1968 I transferred over to Alaska Airlines as their air freight agent for a while, then was sent to Seattle for two weeks of training as a ticket agent and worked in that capacity for a short time. I again transferred back into the air freight department, becoming air freight supervisor from November 1968 to 1971 when Alaska Airlines consolidated many of their positions and made a lot of cutbacks in personnel.

In the fall of 1971, I took a job as a Native Counselor at Sheldon Jackson Jr. College, working as a liaison between the Native students and the administration and staff alike. The position was funded by a federal grant and was a huge success helping Native students cope with college life and help to counsel them on any problems they might have. This position lasted through the school year of 1972 and was then abolished because of a lack of federal funding.

I received a long letter from my mother who was still living in Yakutat telling me how sick and tired she was of all the drinking and the abuse she was getting from her live-in male companion. She explained that she had become quite active in the Council on Alcoholism , there in Yakutat and tried several times, though unsuccessful, to quit drinking on her terms, but was having a tough time of it because all of her friends were not supporting her at all; in fact, they were trying to encourage her not to quit and she honestly felt the only way she could quit was to move away completely

She asked if she could stay with us for a while as she tried to straighten out her life. I didn't hesitate at all as I called her and told her to be on the next flight out of Yakutat. I fixed up a room for her in our large upstairs the next day and went out to the airport to meet her. Keep in mind now that I hadn't seen my mother in six years and when she stepped off the plane the next day, I almost didn't recognize her. Alcohol has a way of aging a person fast, well beyond their years.

I took care of her for the next full year trying my best to help her help herself. That is what it takes to win the battle of the bottle. The only way an alcoholic can really actually quit drinking and boozing is when and if the individual seriously wants to quit drinking—and admits that they do have a very real problem and does something very positive to try to quit.

I practically bottle-fed her a half pint of whiskey every other day for the first six months, then it was about once each week, when she finally stopped asking for it on her own. All during this time she would be going to AA meetings almost every night and I was so damn proud of her for her courage and her fortitude! She had a lot of support from people within her own age group and people would call her a lot asking if she wanted company or would she like to go to bingo or a movie or whatever, just to keep her mind off drinking. It became apparent to me after about eight months that Mom was finally going to beat the dreaded disease called alcoholism!

By the end of the first year of her sobriety, she became quite involved in AA meetings and would be out counseling others whenever they needed help or support. She moved into the halfway house on Mt. Edgecumbe and became the cook for the live-in recovering alcoholics. By this time the oil pipeline was being built and I had been drawing unemployment most of the past year, while taking care of Mom until she was able to take care of herself.

Job Services was really looking for people to be trained as clerks or office workers so I chose to take a three-month clerical cluster course in Kenai, Alaska. This was actually a beginning typing course. I had completed about three weeks of training when I was offered a job as a Native Camp Counselor by Alyeska Pipeline Company, a position very similar to the one I had in Sheldon Jackson Jr. College.

I feel I've got to digress here a bit and explain that from the time I left Yakutat in 1965 to the present I was having very severe marital problems. It seemed that our problems evolved around money; that is, not making enough to meet our monthly bills. Although we kept our problems low profile, my wife's constant drinking became a real nightmare for me. We now had-four children to raise and my two older sons were fourteen and thirteen, my daughter was eleven, and my youngest was nine.

My wife kept her job at the Mt. Edgecumbe Hospital as an LPN, but I felt that if she kept her lifestyle she might soon be terminated. I began to hear rumors that she had a friend that lived out on Halibut Point Road and even received a couple of phone calls from friends of mine who told me they had had several close calls while driving in from the ferry terminal. She apparently was hitchhiking back home from her friend's house and almost got hit by them a couple of times. This was why I felt that maybe if I was finally able to make enough money to take care of our financial obligations things might just work out for us as a family.

I was never so wrong in my entire life! I spent six months working on the pipeline and sent home my paychecks every Friday in the amount of $1,200 and all I got were letters asking for more money.

In December 1974, the main camp where I was stationed shut down because of a big fire that totally destroyed the kitchen facilities for the entire camp. I was sent back home and was immediately hired back at the Pulp Mill under some kind of handicapped program that had just started. By this time, my wife and I both agreed we would seek professional counseling to work out our problems together. That was a real disaster because after our initial first session together, the counselor felt that my wife definitely needed a psychiatric evaluation. This triggered something in her mind about her mother that I wasn't even aware of at the time. Her mother had been recently admitted to an institution in Anchorage because of severe brain damage due to drinking.

However heartbreaking it must have been for her to be carrying this burden of knowing her mother was in an institution, I felt she should have at least told me about it. Now I know and feel that I was as much to blame for our situation as anyone because my wife was always a happy, partying type of person who loved to dance and was the center of attention whenever we did go out to dance. I was a real party-pooper. Just trying my best to take her out dancing as much as I could; however, each time we did go out she would leave me at a table by myself most of the time. She would ask others to dance because at the time I only danced slow dances. I would eventually leave and go home because I would be so embarrassed.

Let these words be a warning to all—live life according to God's plan.

Tomorrow

Have you ever wondered what tomorrow may bring?
It may bring sadness, or gladness
according to God's plan.
Like news of the loss of a relative so far-far away,
Or the happiness of knowing
your daughter is having twins.
Life is too short to dwell on the negative side of things.
It must be lived to the fullest extent possible.
You must do all you can possibly do while you can.
But remember this warning,
It must be according to God's plan.
Do not be reckless or careless and take care of your body,
It's the only one you have and spare parts
are not readily available.
Before going to sleep tonight, plan for tomorrow,
And follow through with whatever you plan to do.
I say these things because I know that tomorrow
Will bring nothing but darkness for me, you see.
I lived life with reckless abandonment and didn't care.
I drank too much and was driving home last night.
They tell me I drove right off a bridge into a deep gorge.
The doctor has just left my bedside and he
Has told me there will never ever
be another tomorrow for me.
Let these words of truth and wisdom be a warning to all.
Live life to the fullest, but live it according to God's plan!

25

Peggy's Death

I was at work at the Pulp Mill at about twelve-thirty on a Saturday afternoon. I just finished my lunch when I saw this Police Officer come into the office area where I was working. He spoke with someone near the door and I saw the guy pointing in my direction. I seemed to sense something had happened to my wife. I thought she may have gotten picked up and was in jail or something. However, I certainly wasn't prepared to hear what the officer told me. He came up to me and asked me if I was Walter Adams and if my wife's name was Peggy.

I said, "Yes, why? Is she in jail or something?"

He said, "No, Mr. Adams, but I'm afraid I have some bad news for you." He continued on after asking me to please sit down. "I don't quite know how to tell you this, but your wife was hit by an automobile last night, and I'm afraid she's dead!"

I was in such shock and disbelief after hearing what this officer just told me. My whole body went numb and my mind went blank for a while as I wept like a baby. After allowing me some time to compose myself, the officer asked if I wanted him to drive me home. I thanked him for the offer, but assured him I would be able to drive myself home after a while.

It was still early in the afternoon so all my kids would still be at home watching cartoons. I barely remember the drive to town because all I was thinking about was how I was going to tell my kids. Before leaving the pulp mill I called my mother, who worked at the halfway house on Mt. Edgecumbe Island, to meet me at my house in about a half hour or so. I told her what had happened and wanted her to be with all of us when I told my children the news.

Finally arriving home, my kids were all gathered around the T.V. watching cartoons. I entered, trying to act as if nothing had happened. I told my kids I wasn't feeling well and took the rest of the day off. I was just stalling for time, waiting for my mother to arrive so I could tell my kids the terrible news.

Mom finally arrived and was doing her best to act as if nothing had happened. As she entered the house I immediately went over to the T.V. set and turned it off, telling the kids I wanted them all to sit at the table. I told them I had something very important to tell them. I had three sons and a daughter.

My oldest son was fourteen, my middle son thirteen, my daughter was eleven and my youngest son nine. I barely remember what or how I said it, but it went something like this. I said, "I don't quite know how to tell you kids, but your mother won't be coming home today or any other day. She was hit by a car last night and was killed instantly."

We immediately all went into a huddle in the middle of the living room, just hugging each other, sobbing so sorrowfully for what seemed like an eternity.

We were finally jolted to our senses by the telephone ringing. It was the mortuary calling for me, telling me I had to come up to identify my wife's body.

I can tell you that nothing can ever prepare a person to identify another person, especially when it is your own wife! Anyway, I did what I had to do and will not elaborate further. I eventually came home and it seemed like the next few days were just a blur in my mind. I barely remember the memorial and burial services because I felt as if I was in a completely different place and time, except I know the hurt my kids were going through.

As the days turned into weeks, my kids kept asking me "Why did Mommy have to die?" I could not give them any kind of a satisfactory answer except to try to comfort them by saying I was as much at fault because I wasn't more understanding or something to that effect. I used to take the kids for long rides, sometimes packing a lunch and staying out all day just to get out of the house and away from it all.

I soon found myself floundering and trying to lose myself in alcohol. Would you believe that my mom was the one that made me snap out of it real fast? Of course, I never was much of a drinker at any time anyway, but it has a cruel way of sneaking up on you real fast. I found myself going out more and actually drinking more than I used to, but Mom told me something that really hit home.

She sat me down one time about two weeks after Peggy had died and told me that I was the one that helped her overcome alcohol. She certainly didn't want to see me become a real alcoholic like she was. She stated, matter-of-factly, that if I didn't straighten myself up she would have no reason to stay sober and would start to drink again. She made me promise her that I would stop my drinking. Now I don't know if it was a bluff on her part or not, but it certainly worked. I soon straightened up my life and put all my energy into taking care of my children and fixing up the house.

Peggy had had an insurance policy where she worked, and indemnity. I was able to pay the mortgage on the house and pay off all our outstanding bills. I also began to refurnish the interior of our house with new furniture, etc.

I can say that as time passes things do get easier and better, depending on how one's outlook is. Anyway, I finally resigned from the pulp mill and in the fall of 1975 took a job as a cook's helper at the Mt. Edgecumbe Boarding School at Mt. Edgecumbe, Alaska.

I had been working for just about a year when I first met Arlene. I met Arlene in 1976 when she brought her sister, Josephine, over to Sitka for a weekend getaway. I honestly felt that fate had brought us both together at a time when we each needed to share the feelings of our recent losses.

Arlene had lost her husband, a pilot, in an airplane crash in Juneau during the first part of 1975. His name was James Masse. They had three young boys. I lost my wife in April of 1975 and I had three young boys and a daughter.

When I first saw Arlene it was love at first sight for me. Cupid's arrow hit me deep in the center of my heart. We talked for hours about our recent losses and how ironic it was that we should meet. I especially loved how her eyes seemed to light up and sparkle whenever she smiled. That night I learned how to fast dance for the first time because Arlene kept telling me to dance with her sister. She thought I was interested in her! I really only wanted to dance with Arlene, but I was the perfect gentleman and must have danced every dance fast or slow for about a four-hour period before we finally left and had an early breakfast.

Since they were going back to Juneau the next day I offered to drive them to the airport, which I did. As they boarded the plane I knew in my heart that this would not be the last time I would be seeing Arlene.

Soon days turned into weeks and although the weekends were the loneliest times for me I would keep busy with the kids. We would go on picnics or long drives in the evenings or see a good movie together.

By now, Arlene and I were corresponding quite frequently, either by letters or by telephone. I soon found myself making weekend trips to Juneau to visit her and her family.

Arlene's parents, Joe and Alice Bennett, have been a great blessing to us throughout our marriage and continue to this day.

Their Christian love and support have been strength in our lives. I have come to love and respect them for their deep understanding of family values. They are both in their mid-eighties and have been married for well over sixty years, having raised five sons and two daughters in a very secure loving relationship.

I just love the many occasions when the whole family gets together to celebrate someone's birthday or an anniversary or some holiday at their home. Even the smallest occasion turns out to be a real feast for all because there are so many of us. There is always plenty of food for everyone and these occasions give Mom and Pop time to visit with their grandchildren. It isn't unusual to have an average of about twenty or more of us family members gathered together for a typical dinner.

Pop usually starts each gathering by explaining why we are gathered together and before eating, he blesses the food with a prayer. Sometimes Pop will mention that these last few years have been their "bonus" years together. I would like to thank them both for being able to share their bonus years together with their family. I wish them both many more blessed bonus years together with their family.

I finally proposed to Arlene and she accepted my proposal, so in 1977, I sold my house in Sitka and moved to Juneau.

Oh, by the way, I never did mention her kids. She had three boys: James 10, Brian 8, and John 6. My three boys were Walter Jr. 16, Richard 15, and Michael 10. My daughter was twelve at the time and her name is Dorinda. We were the real "Brady Bunch," only we soon became the "Adams Family." Anyone that can add can tell that seven kids in one household can be a real trying experience.

Arlene sold her home on Behrends Avenue in Juneau and we bought a house on Second Street in Douglas, Alaska. We were officially married on May 20, 1977.

I worked for the Tlingit and Haida Community Council,

becoming involved in Native community affairs, settling in for what was a very trying time for our entire family. My wife, Arlene, was really having a time at home keeping law and order around the house. We used to fold down the back seat of our station wagon and all seven of our kids would somehow squeeze in and off we'd go, anywhere, just to get everybody out of the house.

This one time we stopped off at Arlene's parents' house on Glacier Avenue for a short visit. When we were ready to continue our ride everyone jumped into our car and we took off, heading out toward the end of the road, or so we thought. About halfway out to the end of the road, someone said, "Where's Brian?" We had completely forgotten to take a head count as we all left Arlene's parents' house and left Brian behind. He was just lying on floor by the T.V. set, as happy as ever, watching cartoons. He didn't even realize he was supposed to come with us when we all left. Another incident I remember real well happened on a Saturday afternoon. We left all the kids at home because they were all watching cartoons and Arlene and I needed to do our grocery shopping. We were probably gone for about three hours and surprised everyone when we did return.

We walked into our house and I tell you, it looked like a monsoon had struck the inside of our house. All the kids had a water fight, chasing each other around, throwing cups of water at each other. Well needless to say, everyone was grounded for a week, and it took all of them a whole hour to clean up the mess they made.

I'd like to tell you a little about my wife's health problems. She has overcome many "severe" crisis situations in her life. I'm sure you'll agree and understand why I am so thankful for having her.

Arlene's medical problems began as a young child in her teens. She developed whooping cough, which causes her respira-

158

tory problems. Mainly with her left lung. She was sent to Mt. Edgecumbe Hospital where she spent almost a year. The doctors operated on her to remove a quarter-size portion of her left lung. However, while in surgery, the doctors nicked an artery, which complicated matters to where she had to have her whole left lung removed! Since then, her heart and stomach have been pushed over to the left side, trying to fill in the area where her lung was. This has caused quite a strain on her heart and has caused a curvature of her spine at the back of her neck. This causes her severe shoulder pain on her left shoulder, as well as severe digestive-tract problems.

She also developed several thyroid nodules in her thyroid gland. These have all been benign and two of them have been surgically removed. They have since treated her thyroid gland with radiation to kill the growth of any more nodules.

She had gallstones removed and has had surgery to repair a tear in her stomach lining along the scar tissue of her scar for the removal of her left lung.

Also, beginning in 1985, at the age of forty-five, she had developed severe asthma and allergy problems. I am certain that she has probably spent more time in the hospital than out between the years of 1984 to 2002. She seems to have stabilized for the last couple of years and has not had a severe asthma attack for quite a while.

She is indeed a medical marvel because she was told that she could never have children because the strain would be too much for her. She has proven them all wrong and I again thank God for having her.

Children's Rights

In my day it was unheard of to talk back to your parents
For any reason. It just wasn't the thing to do.
What has caused children to change so drastically?
To where they now tell their parents what to do
And where to go and how we can get there too?
They now have the right to do whatever they
Want to do, whenever they want to do it, and
There's not a thing we, as parents, can do to stop
Them, because they have their rights too.
Children have lost the meaning of the phrase
"Love, Honor and Obey your parents at all times."
This is why so many younger children are
Running away from home, living on the streets, etc.
Parents cannot cope with a teenager who will
Not abide by any rules in the home, so there's no
Recourse, but to put them in foster homes,
Or whatever.
I say give parents their rights back as parents!

26

Across Country on Vacation
with All Seven Children

Sometime during the first year in 1977, we went on a vacation all the way to northern Michigan to meet Arlene's former in-laws. All nine of us flew to Seattle, then took a bus all the way to Milwaukee, Wisconsin, then caught a ferry across the lake to Muskegon, Michigan. It took three and a half days of traveling across the country.

I had never been on vacation before and I had never traveled practically across the U.S. before either, so this was a whole new experience for me. I remember trying to sleep on the bus, rocking back and forth, just barely bumping heads with the other passengers across the aisle from me, and then waking myself up with a loud snore. I felt as if everyone on the whole bus heard me.

There was this one couple that sat directly behind me and one of them kept singing this song, "Just-a-Swinging." We had to listen to that same song for two whole nights and believe me, I couldn't get that tune out of my head for a long time.

One night, near Chicago, my wife woke up and asked me, "Where are we?" I didn't have the foggiest idea where we were, but glanced out of the bus window and saw a large sign that was all lit up. It was a Conoco gas station.

Now this goes to show you that I came right out of the "sticks" because I told her, "I think we just passed a town called Con-oh-co." She didn't say a word about it until the next day while passing through a large town. She was looking out the bus window when all of a sudden she burst out in laughter. She saw a Conoco sign and explained to me that it was the name of a gas station or sort of like a franchise.

Wait now, because there's still more to come.

The next day I saw this sign at a car dealership, HYUNDAI, and asked my wife what kind of car is HIGH-UN-DAY? Wait now; this still isn't the end of it.

She pretended she didn't hear me I guess because she didn't even respond. Later on the same day we passed another service station that had a large SUNOCO sign by it, and my wife came up with this saying for me. She told me that only I could live in a town called CON-OH-CO and drive a HIGH-UN-DAY that uses SUNOCO fuel. I really had to laugh at that one.

You know, we finally did arrive in Michigan, but to be honest with you, I never thought we'd ever get out of Montana. We all must have looked a sight, all rugged looking, each one of the kids packing their sleeping bags. We probably looked like illegal aliens come to pick cherries.

We had a great two-week vacation and met all of Arlene's former in-laws. We must have traveled to every part of the Upper Peninsula during the first week.

One day, we went through an agate shop in Grand Marias, Michigan and bought several pieces of jewelry for gifts. After we got back to our hotel room, we noticed our two youngest sons were taking these nice colored rocks out of their pockets and putting them in a pile on the bed. Well, we found out they had picked up about four pounds of agates from that little shop. We immediately scolded them and I called the agate shop to explain what our boys did. The next day we returned those agates and had the boys apologize to the owner.

We rented a large station wagon during the last week we were there. Before we returned it I pulled into a car wash. It was the kind where you put money into a machine and grab hold of a hose and it dispenses soapy water. The one I chose had a hole in the hose, just about eye level. I put my money in and turned the crank and was just reaching for the hose as the water pressure made the hose start jumping around, swaying back and forth like a snake, all the while spraying me with soapy water.

It caught me completely off guard and as my wife and kids were all hysterical, sitting in the car just laughing at me and watching me chasing this hose back and forth, giving me a good shower. I finally did catch the hose and managed to wash the dust and dirt off the car, but by the time I was through I was soaking wet. That was the first and last time I ever got a shower and car wash at the same time. We all laughed at that incident for quite a while.

The time finally arrived when we had to say good-bye and return back to civilization again. We settled back into our home in Douglas and soon felt the wrath of the Taku winds, as we prepared for our first winter living in Douglas.

I had a small, black cocker spaniel/poodle mix dog by the name of Lady. She had thick fur that had to be brushed almost constantly. She was an outside dog and used to sleep alongside the concrete steps in the back of the house. One night we had a lot of snow overnight with high winds, causing high snow drifts. Late in the afternoon the kids kept telling Arlene they couldn't find Lady. She had been out all night and all day, and it had snowed about two feet already.

When I came home from work, I went out back and called for her without any response. I tried again about an hour later, and had all but given up, when I saw this large mound of snow start to move. Pretty soon Lady appeared out of the mound, and starts shaking the snow off, a little slow in her walk, but apparently fine as she ate a large meal and drank plenty of water.

Another night during that first cold spell, we decided to

build a fire in our fireplace. I went down to the garage to chop some kindling and bring up some larger pieces of split wood. When I returned, all the kids were gathered around the fireplace, just waiting for me to build our first fire. Someone said they had opened the damper so I didn't even double-check to make certain it was open as I proceeded to build a nice fire. I lit the bundle of newspapers and all seemed to be doing fine as the flames were really getting higher and higher, and the smoke wasn't going up the chimney, but coming out toward the ceiling. By now all the kids were running to their rooms as I realized the damper wasn't open at all.

My oldest son kept running up and down the stairs shouting, "The hose!" but doing nothing about it because he was in such a panic.

By this time the flames started shooting out and up the front of the mantle toward the ceiling. I knew if I didn't do something fast, we'd have a real fire going. I ran to the sink and filled a pot with water and poured it directly on the fire and managed to completely douse the flames with a second pot of water.

Needless to say, the damper was not open, but closed. Later that evening we had a major talk with all the children making them understand what the damper is and why it has to be open, etc.

Our second year of marriage settled down quite a bit because due to attrition I only had my youngest son and my three step-sons living with us.

My youngest son was a real problem child for us, doing almost everything within his power to disrupt our marriage in some way. It took a counselor only one session to identify the real problem. I was the real culprit because I allowed him to get me mad and when he did that, he was getting all the attention he wanted, even if it was a spanking or whatever.

He moved to Sitka in the beginning of the school year in

1980 to live with a family that we knew, because he wouldn't live by our rules.

My stepsons have never been a problem for me at all. In fact, they each accepted me right from the start simply because they were still quite young when their dad died. As far as they were concerned, I was their dad now and that's the way it's been ever since.

My youngest son, John, and I really bonded during this period in his life and it was great for me as it was for him because we needed each other.

True friends will always be there for you if they are true, indeed.

Friends

True friends will never ever forsake you
They will always be there for you in time of need.
Have you ever tried to quit a bad habit?
Like drinking or maybe smoking cigarettes?
You thought all your friends would support you,
But instead, those so-called friends tried
To keep you from quitting
in order to support their habit.
Over time you will prevail
and know who your real friends are.
The ones who support you are still by your side,
While the ones you supported while drinking are gone.
Therein lies the difference between all so-called friends.

27

Moving to Seattle

I continued working for the Juneau Tlingit & Haida Community Council until May of 1986. Due to many personal conflicts with the chairman of the Community Council, who was my direct supervisor, I was terminated and subsequently became embroiled in defending myself against a claim of mismanagement. This claim was finally dropped and I feel I exonerated myself of any wrongdoing, but the whole process made me so bitter I don't want anything more to do with Native politics.

I immediately found employment with the Juneau Cold Storage Company as an office assistant for the next two summers. Ocean Beauty Seafoods Company (a subsidiary of Sealaska Corporation) was my employer, holding the lease on the facilities at the cold storage. We sold ice and purchased fish from the local fishermen in the Juneau area, mainly from the gillnetters. Ocean Beauty Seafoods finally shut down the whole operation at Juneau Cold Storage, and I soon found myself being offered a job as an inventory clerk with Seattle Seafoods Company in Seattle, Washington.

Seattle Seafoods Company is another subsidiary of Sealaska Corporation. I was interviewed for the job via telephone and felt a little uneasy about accepting the position, simply because I was told I would be working with a computer all day long, five days a week.

I informed my employer that I didn't know a thing about

computers and, in fact, had never touched one before. Their reply was this: "Well, you'll learn real fast then, huh?"

I accepted the challenge and we moved to Seattle in August of 1986. My wife and three boys didn't join me until November because they had to pack up everything in the house and have all our belongings shipped to Seattle, thinking we were making a lengthy stay. My wife arranged for her brother to move into our house and continue making house payments rather than to rent or lease it to someone.

I lasted for about three months in that position before I realized I wasn't the computer whiz my employer thought I could be.

I transferred out of that position and accepted a clean-up position in the processing department, hosing down the whole processing plant after hours when the plant was shut down for the night.

To make a long story short, I became a virtual slave to the management of Sealaska Seafoods Company, doing more and more work as time went by and not getting paid for the overtime hours I was putting in. I became frustrated and a little bit mouthy with the management because they wouldn't hire another person to help the two of us out so we could in fact get the job done within the time frame we were given, that I finally told them to take the job and shove it, literally.

I drew unemployment for the next six months while trying to find meaningful work. My mother came down for a medical check-up and stayed with us for about two weeks. It was during this visit that she found out she had developed a lymph-node cancer and it was spreading fast! She had been given just six months to live!

Mom was very strong and accepted the fact that if it was God's will that she be taken away, she could continue to live her remaining days as she wanted to. She returned to Sitka and quietly made arrangements to move to the Sitka Pioneer's Home when she felt she needed to and bought a burial plot at Sitka Cemetery and completed her will.

Return Home

I had applications out all over Seattle and was about to give up all hope of ever finding a job when I was notified by an employment office that a large janitorial company was hiring a lot of maintenance people for many of the high-rise office buildings in downtown Seattle. Well, two days later I was working for Wright Runstad Co., doing janitorial and maintenance work in a high-rise building in what is now called the City Bank Building in downtown Seattle.

I really enjoyed the work and immediately worked my way up the ladder and became their number-one employee, putting in as much overtime as I could handle. I honestly believe if I had stayed with that position I would have become a supervisor probably within two years and I'm not bragging either, just stating a fact.

However, we received word in the spring of 1989 that Arlene's father had had a stroke and it was a severe shock to Arlene, not being there with him. We immediately made arrangements to come back home so Arlene could be with her parents if anything happened to her dad. I had just returned from Sitka a week earlier to attend Mom's funeral.

We returned back home from Seattle on June 28, 1989, and although Arlene's father recovered from his stroke quite well, we were all just thankful to be back home again living in our own house in Douglas. The economy in the Juneau area seemed to be on the upswing again after the economic crash in the mid-1980s. I soon took a job with City and Borough of Juneau working as a janitor at the Juneau Teen Club. I had applications out all over the Juneau area and received a notice of interview from the State of Alaska to be interviewed as a correctional officer at the State Lemon Creek Correctional Facility.

I can honestly tell you, I was ecstatic and felt that maybe the good Lord was looking out for me after all as I went for my job interview. I was hired and was told to report for duty on December 18, which was just two weeks away.

I immediately put in my notice with the City and Borough of Juneau, and reported for my first day of work as a correctional officer for the State of Alaska on December 18, 1989.

During the early part of 2001, Pop had become quite ill. He developed chronic lung problems which required him to use oxygen constantly. He soon became bedridden, and as sick as he was, he still had a good sense of humor. was trying in his own way to show his family that he still needed them around during family get-togethers. The whole family used to gather around his bed to hear him tell us some story or to relate something of importance concerning all of us.

He never did make it to celebrate his sixty-fifth wedding anniversary. He passed away peacefully on September 9, 2002, without any suffering at all!

We all miss him so very much and can assure you it will take a long time for all of us to get over our loss.

Falling stars are much more than wishing stars falling from the sky. They can be the whole truth.

Wishes

I wished upon a falling star, once upon a time
My wish came true though, it wasn't really mine
It was for you, Dad, that wish I wished that night
You were so frail and weak, you could hardly speak
But the voice I heard sounded like a mockingbird
On that fateful day in May
when my dad had passed away
Since that fateful day in May,
Mom has since been taken away
A second wish that I have wished has since come true
Now whenever I look up in the sky at night
As promised, I can always see, with delight
Their faces, smiling down at me, from heaven above.

28

My Personal Comments

I'd like to tell you a little bit of the personal side of me and how my life changed for the better since I lost my leg.

I can say now, simply because I have no way of knowing what kind of person I would be right now, but my accident truly made me see the light, so to speak. My whole outlook on life completely changed because I believe God has a plan for us here on earth and whatever that plan is, there is not a thing that we can do to change that.

You know, it is kind of like worrying so much about not being able to pay your bills for the month and you develop an ulcer because of it. No matter how much you worry about it though, the bills are still there—unless you pay them.

I can honestly say right now, and at this time, I am content and at peace with myself because I have a good job and am finally making enough money to pay the bills and I have a good health insurance plan and can look forward to having a good retirement income.

My Tlingit name is Yucha-haatch and the only interpretation of what it means as far as I know is Smiling Mountain. I have always been very proud to be given that name because it fits me perfectly. I have always thought of myself as being a happy, smiling person.

I mentioned previously I have always had nicknames throughout my life. I'd like to mention how I was given the name of Popeye. My brother, Bertrand Adams, is four years older than I, and when we moved from Sitka to Yakutat, I was only about a month old. Apparently, after Mom and Dad got married, Dad had asked my brother one day what they were going to call me. I was told the song "Popeye the Sailor Man" was quite popular, and I believe Dad used to hold me in his arms and sing that song to me—so all my brother could think of was Popeye I guess—so that nickname stuck with me.

It isn't a coincidence then that as I got older and was just starting to talk I was asked what we should call my brother, Bert. The song "Pennies from Heaven" was another popular song at the time and Mom always used to sing me to sleep with that song I guess. I was told that I was fussy and sleepy at the time so all I wanted was for Mom to sing the song "Pennies from Heaven" to me. All I could say was penny, I guess—so that was how my brother, Bert, got his nickname of Penny. Isn't it kind of amazing how we seem to just accept these kinds of things and take them for granted, but it becomes a very interesting subject when explained in detail?

Popeye stuck with me until I moved away from Yakutat and I have since been given all different kinds of nicknames. Some of them I'd like to mention, but can't because my conscience won't allow me to. However, some of the more fitting ones have been "Slim" and "Two-by-Four" because I am of small build, sorta shaped like a tree, but as solid as a two by four. I am purely speculating here now and giving you my own interpretation because I've never asked anyone else for their reason why they call me some name, because I prefer to keep that to myself. I feel I have the privilege of making my own interpretation.

I have been working at Lemon Creek Correctional Facility a little over fourteen years now and have acquired the nickname of "Splinter." My fellow co-workers named me "Splinter" because I am always telling someone of some embarrassing incident that happened to me over the years regarding my prosthesis. I won't elaborate further because you'll find out why a little later on.

Splinter does fit me well because it has a more mature wooden sound to it, don't you think? I've also been called "Stick," but I think I prefer Splinter.

I'm sure I can say that those of you that know me will probably have to agree that I am a rather shy, sensitive individual with a deep sense of caring for other people. I would now like to tell you that I began to have health problems in July of 2001. I had been having problems urinating and went through all kinds of tests. The doctors thought it was my prostate gland; however, the different tests ruled out any problem with my prostate gland. So they began to look elsewhere for my ailment.

I was now urinating blood on a regular basis. Finally on about the twelfth of August, the doctors found a very large tumor that had completely invaded my right kidney. I was told I had to have immediate surgery to have my whole right kidney removed. I ended up going to Virginia Mason Hospital in Seattle and was scheduled for surgery August 23, 2001!

I was never ever afraid for my life because I knew in my heart that I would recover and be just fine. I don't know why, but I just did!

The surgery went fine and the doctors said they got all of the tumor out. I am now doing just fine and can truthfully say that I am a true cancer survivor!

I would like to close my life story now with a prayer of thanks to the good Lord for allowing me to live a very unique life and have the ability to tell you about my life, while I still can.

We can never thank the Lord enough for giving us life to enjoy all of life's pleasures.

A Prayer of Thanks

I thank you, Lord, for saving my soul
For sparing my life and making me whole
To live and to love, so my dreams can come true
In your wonderful world of red, white and blue.
For my wife and children we have to share,
For the many burdens and heartaches we must bear.
I thank you, Lord, for creating the earth,
For all life forms and the miracle of birth.
For the highest mountains and the valleys so low,
For the sun and the moon and stars that glow,
For the trees and grasses and the land and the sea.
But most of all, Lord, I thank you for saving me.

I've always felt that I had a sense of humor, but just never did know how to demonstrate it. I've kept it built in and hidden over the years simply not knowing how to bring it out—until I decided to put it in writing that is. I feel the time is right for the world to meet Splinter.

But first, I must explain that Splinter has become more than just a nickname to me. Splinter has a complete personality all his own and is as real a person as I am, in my mind at least.

In my mind my prosthesis is the real Splinter, as it comes to life and tells me all the wild tales of its many adventures in life. If you will remember what I said when I first got my prosthesis in 1963, I said I never did consider myself to be handicapped at all, just a little disadvantaged. With these thoughts in mind then, please remember Splinter's law, "If you cannot laugh at yourself, who can you laugh at?"

I believe it is good therapy for everyone to be able to laugh at themselves, if for no other reason than to make life a little more bearable to people who may be a little more disadvantaged than I.

Splinter's Memories

I would like to dedicate this episode of "Splinter's Memories" to my wife, Arlene, for understanding who "Splinter" is, allowing me to laugh at myself, and for putting up with me for more than twenty-five years!

I Love You—To My Wife, Arlene

"I love you" are just words, but words we like to hear
I'll go a step further and tell you why I love you
You have an aura that attracts me like a magnet
Your dimples are like dewdrops on your cheeks
Your eyes light up and sparkle whenever you smile
You have a heart of gold; you are the apple of my eye
You are my lawyer; my teacher; my reason for living
You care more about others than about yourself
You'd gladly give an arm or a leg to make someone happy
Even if you are having problems of your own
So now, my love, my dear and loving wife
It is time for you to have and take
These simple words of truth straight to your heart
And know these words I write are from my own
I could go on and on; there are many more reasons
But most of all, I love you because you're you.

Splinter

An Introduction

Splinter is my name and laughter is my game
I may be small of stature and built like a tree
Sort of narrow at the shoulders
and a little wide at the hips
I can kick like a mule and float like a cork
Yeah, I've done it all, I can't complain
I mooned the moon on occasion and got quite hot,
Embarrassed, if you will, at the lesson it taught
Not to take on a dare, during a full moon
I'm even known to have made this claim to fame
Of touching the ceiling with one foot while keeping
The other foot flat on the floor—figure that one out
Though I may seem kind of quiet and shy
I love to see people laugh at my humor and wit
Because humor to me, is like good medicine you see
Whenever you see Splinter—please laugh with me.

Float Like a Cork

In the spring of 1965, just before I put the padlock on my café in Yakutat to move back to Sitka, Alaska, I had my first and last experience with wearing hip boots.

I was fishing for king salmon in the Situk River, in an area where the current ran quite swiftly downstream. I was casting out and letting my lure drift downstream with the current. As luck would have it, I snagged a tree stump and couldn't get my lure unstuck. I started to wade out deeper and deeper, trying to get closer to the stump when all of a sudden, my prosthetic leg just pops up out of the water like a cork and I began to float downstream on my back. I felt so darned helpless because, although the water was only about waist deep, I couldn't stand up! I had to paddle back to shore on my back! To this day, I will not wear hip boots . . . even if I do have a built-in life preserver!

Take Me Out to the Ball Game

In 1974, my youngest son, Michael, who was, nine years old at the time, went with me to a basketball game in Sitka. We were going to watch my fourteen-year-old son, Walter Jr., play in a preliminary game between Sitka and Mt. Edgecumbe Junior Varsity.

The gym was really full and I was apprehensive about leaving my seat to get some refreshments. The concession stand was on the other side of the gym and, as we were making our way through the crowd down off the bleachers, I felt something give way on my prosthesis. As I glanced down to where my foot was supposed to be I realized there was no foot there! At the same instant, I heard a loud crash under the bleacher as my foot made contact with the floor. Well, needless to say, I felt as if every single person in the gym had their eyes glued to me. I was starting to sweat and, in my infinite wisdom, decided to sit right where I was and act as if nothing had ever happened.

Well, Michael, who was walking ahead of me, didn't know a thing about what happened. He was already on the gym floor waving at me with a puzzled look on his face because I wasn't following behind him.

I finally managed to entice him to come back to where I was sitting and explained that my foot broke off. He calmly agreed to retrieve it, and to my utter amazement and surprise, he popped up from under the bleachers down at the other end holding my foot up over his head. Waving it back and forth, he yelled, "I got it, Dad!"

By now, I was practically under the bleachers myself, and without looking in his direction, I heard myself say, "Please, son, wrap it in a bag and bring it to me."

Being Dad's savior and not knowing any better, he came trudging down the aisle waving my foot in front of people's noses. He finally handed me my foot and, inspecting the prosthesis, I found that the bolt that attaches the foot to the ankle had broken completely off!

Well, we came up with a plan of action. As I started scooting down each step of the bleachers toward the gym floor, my son made a beeline for the first-aid station. Just as I reached the last step, he came out of this room pushing a wheelchair. I calmly hopped into the chair and he wheeled me out of the gymnasium amidst the loudest cheers and clapping that I have ever heard.

Hole in One

While shopping at the Northgate Mall in Seattle, Washington in October of 1977, 1 was wearing my favorite pair of slacks that were quite worn. You know the type, where the seat is almost worn through and the front pockets have holes in them, but you just don't want to give them up?

I had a lot of coins in my pocket and had just left my wife, Arlene, at J.C. Penney's and was walking down to the other end of the mall looking for a place to get a cup of coffee.

All of a sudden, I felt a searing pain in my kneecap area and let out this blood-curdling shriek! I literally fell to my knees on the floor thinking I was shot or something!

I immediately had about a dozen people around me offering assistance in some way. After helping me back to my feet and hobbling to the nearest bathroom, I heard a coin drop down to the end of my prosthesis.

Sure enough, it was a nickel that had slipped through the hole in my pocket and lodged itself in front of my kneecap.

Go Ahead, Bite Me

This incident happened not too long after moving into our home in Douglas in 1977.

It was a beautiful Saturday afternoon and I was home all by myself so I decided to walk to the post office to check our mail. I was walking along in front of Mike's Place restaurant on Second Street in Douglas when this large black Labrador comes running up to me. The dog starts barking and snapping at my left leg like he wanted to bite me.

Well, I was feeling quite peppy at the time so I thrust my left leg out toward the dog's head. He snaps at my foot and actually bites into my shoe and begins to twist his head from side to side almost knocking me to the ground.

I kicked forward so hard that my foot finally came out of his mouth, but not before embedding two of his teeth into the toe area of my left shoe. The dog shrieked in pain and slowly whimpered off toward the restaurant.

I'm in no pain as I reach down and retrieve the two teeth from my shoe—which was my prosthetic foot!

Fish On

Upon returning from our vacation in 1977 and settling back into our home in Douglas, I had taken my three stepsons to Fish Creek to catch some silver salmon or cohos. The eldest one was James, who was ten years old; Brian who was eight; and John who was six.

We were all having a great time until James' line got all tangled. John was about 100 feet downstream fighting a salmon, while Brian was about fifteen feet behind me. I was helping James untangle his line, with my back facing Brian, who had just cast his line out into the creek.

I remember hearing Brian holler, "I've got one," as he supposedly had a strike. Well, he snapped that pole so hard that the lure and all popped out of the water. The line made a twanging sound as it sailed through the air and made about three complete wraps around the ankle of my prosthesis.

Finally, with a dull "thwack" the lure embedded itself, mostly to my pant leg, into the shin area of my prosthesis.

Needless to say, Brian let out a shriek so loud, I can still hear his voice echoing in my ears whenever I think of this incident! The look on his face as he screamed, "Aaagghhkkk!" and dropped his pole, running off into the brush, heading back to where my wife, Arlene, was waiting in the car about two hundred yards away.

It really took a lot of consoling and reassuring to get Brian to understand that he didn't hook me in the leg at all. At least not my good leg!

No Blood Lost

This incident happened in 1979, while cutting firewood for our fireplace.

I had been chopping these blocks and stacking the wood in a neat pile along the driveway to our house.

My next-door neighbor decided to come over to introduce himself since we hadn't met before. "Hi, neighbor," he said. "My name is John. I saw you out here chopping wood and wondered if you might need some help here, stacking it up?"

I said, "Hi, I'm Walt and yes, I can use a little help here if you don't mind stacking some wood."

"No problem at all," John said as he began to help me stack the wood in a neat pile.

I had quite a stack piled up and had just started a new block when my neighbor noticed this block had a lot of knots on it. He said, "Be careful with that one. It has some pretty nasty knots in it!"

I simply nodded and said, "Okay," as I raised my ax high overhead and came down hard. With a dull "thud" my ax hit a hard knot and bounced off the block. I was still in the down swing when the ax came "whack" across the shin of my left leg.

My neighbor's eyes seemed to bulge out of their sockets as he dropped his stack of wood in his arms and came rushing over to me. He said, "Oh, my gosh, you've surely split your leg open, haven't you?" I just smiled and assured him that the ax just cut my pants, not my leg. Of course, I had to explain that I wear a below-the-knee prosthesis and that's why I didn't bleed.

What Happened

Would you believe that at the time of this incident, it had been thirty-two years since my amputation and I still forgot!

I was working the day shift at the Lemon Creek Correctional Facility in Juneau, Alaska. I worked twelve-hour days, seven days on, seven days off. I had to be to work by five A.M., so I had set my alarm for four-thirty A.M. When my alarm went off, I had to go to the bathroom real bad so I turned on my bedside lamp, threw off the covers, took one step forward and fell flat on my face!

I came down so hard on the end of my stump! I was rolling around on the floor, cursing and crying with the pain!

I had completely forgotten that I had to either hop or put my prosthesis on before I took that first step!

I've Fallen, And . . .

One Saturday afternoon I decided I was going to scrape the moss off our roof in Douglas, Alaska. I had this old rickety six-foot wooden stepladder that should have been thrown out long ago. I positioned this ladder on the concrete porch in the back of our house.

I threw some scrapers and a few other tools I needed up onto the roof and proceeded to climb this ladder to get myself onto the roof. I made it just to the top rung of the ladder and was starting to position my right leg up over the rain gutter when I felt the ladder start to wiggle. I knew I was going to fall straight down onto the concrete porch below me, so I instinctively pushed myself out and away from the roof as far as I could as I started to fall. I was hoping I would land on the grassy lawn instead of the concrete porch below me.

Well, I must have broken through the top three rungs or steps of the ladder as I fell, because my body landed in the backyard, but not before my left leg (my prosthesis) landed across the last stair of the concrete porch. My prosthesis broke completely off right where the end of my stump fits into the socket, about eight inches below my kneecap!

I apparently blacked out for a few minutes because I was in a daze as I sat up, looking at my broken foot lying about a foot away from me in the grass. My left hand was hurting real bad and it looked like two of my fingers might have been broken. My elbow was scratched and I had a scrape on my forehead, but other than that I wasn't seriously hurt.

My wife didn't even know I fell as I came hopping into the house from the back door carrying my foot under my arm. I must have looked a terrible mess, looking at my twisted fingers of my left hand, while asking my wife to get my spare prosthesis out of the closet for me.

After the initial shock of my fall sank in, she managed to drive me out to the clinic where my two fingers were snapped back into place and my scrapes were attended to.

I must tell you I didn't even mention a thing to anyone about my broken prosthesis, but it is a good thing I did have a spare one, huh? How would anyone ever believe me?

I Believe

There is no real death here on earth for any of us
These bodies are but a vessel on loan to us for awhile
We live in a spiritual world after our earthly bodies die
We go toward the bright light willingly and peacefully
It means a whole new beginning
for each and every one of us
A master plan has been laid down by a higher power
You can call it God, Master, Creator,
or whatever you want
Our destiny here on Earth is not controlled by mankind
It lies in the hand of a much greater power than ours
It waits for our development as humans to be complete
Some bits and pieces of the puzzle
are just now being implanted
We're slowly being programmed
to absorb and understand the truth
When we are young, we are shielded from death and sorrow
Parents tell us a loved one is just asleep to ease our pain
We cannot understand the why of it all
and do not question why
Till we grow old ourselves
and the shadow of death approaches us
We are ready and welcome death with open arms
When our heart stops pumping
this lifeblood through our veins.

I'm sure you haven't heard the last of Splinter, as I'm still searching the cosmos, looking for answers to many unanswered questions.

So, until we meet again, always remember to keep a smile on your face and a warm place in your heart.

—Best Wishes,
Walter "Splinter" Adams